TEACH YOURSELF BOOKS

NUTRITION

This book aims to provide a simple, practical introduction to nutrition, a science that deals with what foods are made of and how their different components function in the body. A knowledge of what constitutes a good diet is important not only to people who are professionally concerned with catering, such as those who provide school or hospital meals, but also to mothers who are responsible for feeding a family and to the general reader, who is constantly subjected to propaganda encouraging him to eat one kind of food rather than another and needs to be able to judge for himself.

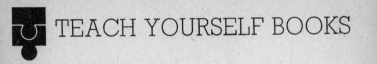
TEACH YOURSELF BOOKS

NUTRITION

Magnus Pyke

ST. PAUL'S HOUSE WARWICK LANE LONDON EC4P 4AH

First printed 1961
This impression 1973

ISBN 0 340 05672 X

Printed Offset Litho in Great Britain for
The English Universities Press Ltd.
by Cox & Wyman Ltd., London, Fakenham and Reading

CONTENTS

PREFACE

ALMOST every person you meet has his own views about food and diet. There are people who think that eating beef steak makes them strong, there are others who believe that white bread is a poison, others again have the idea that if they eat plenty of oranges during the winter they will never catch a cold. One of the most remarkable things that has happened during our lifetime has been the virtual disappearance of babies with rickets and the increased stature and physique of children. Great advances in public health have occurred through the increased knowledge of what constitutes a good diet. This is the science of nutrition.

In this book, I have tried to describe what foods are made of and how their different components function in the body. If you read it you will see that there is no "best" diet but that a good diet can be made up in many different ways. The important thing is that the mixture of foods you choose to eat should add up to the right amount of a number of different nutrients.

The Western world in this century became richer and most people are now able to buy and eat a sufficient diet. In the less fortunate parts of the world, however, the peoples have become poorer as we have become better off, and there are very large numbers of people who cannot obtain enough of the right foods to eat and who suffer from malnutrition. The reason for this can be understood from what has been set out here.

A knowledge of nutrition is important to everyone who takes a serious interest in food. This not only includes people who are professionally concerned with catering, such as those who provide school or hospital meals, but mothers also who are responsible for feeding a family. In another way this book may be useful to the general reader. We are all of us subjected to advertising and propaganda of different kinds encouraging us to eat one kind of food rather than another. A knowledge of the principles of nutrition will, I hope, help people to judge whether claims which are put forward are, in fact, reasonable or not.

During the war of 1939–1945 and under the stimulation of working with the late Sir Jack Drummond at the Ministry of Food, I was given the task of writing a simple text on nutrition which subsequently appeared in print. In writing this present book I should like to acknowledge the assistance derived from the information taken from the "Manual of Nutrition" published by Her Majesty's Stationery Office in 1945 (revised edition 1961).

M.P.

Cambus, Clackmannanshire,
  Scotland

CHAPTER ONE

WHAT NUTRITION IS ABOUT

FOOD is anything that nourishes the body. Nutrition is the science that deals with all the various factors of which food is composed and the way in which proper nourishment is brought about. There is, however, one more side to human nutrition. It is concerned with the feeding of people. In learning about human nutrition, we have, therefore, to consider three things: food, the way in which food is digested, absorbed and used in the tissues of the body, and the kind of people for whom the food is intended.

In the different parts of the world there are all sorts of people, with different tastes, different habits and different kinds of diets cooked in an enormous variety of ways. Even within a single small county there may be different food habits in different districts: in Scotland they eat porridge and like fresh-baked morning rolls, in Wales they eat leeks, in Yorkshire they like high tea and Yorkshire pudding, and in England generally fish and chips are popular articles of diet which, on the other hand, are never eaten in France just across the Channel. Without a proper understanding of the principles of nutrition it is impossible for anyone to know whether the many habits and prejudices which affect what people eat are soundly based or not. Some local habits are useful and have good reasons behind them, others may be harmful and based on mere tradition. "A little of what you fancy does you good" may sometimes be true, but very often it is not.

Whether or not a man comes from Yorkshire, Scotland,

1

Timbuktu or China and whatever dietary customs he was brought up to he is still a member of the human race, that is to say he belongs to the animal species *Homo sapiens*. The science of nutrition, being a branch of applied physiology, takes little account of the subjective feelings of the people being fed. Nutritional well-being is as little affected by the likes and dislikes of whoever is eating a particular diet as are the nutritional requirements of experimental rats confined in a laboratory.

From the rigid standpoint of animal physiology, the average nutritional requirements of groups of people are fixed and depend on such measurable characteristics as sex, age, height, weight, degree of activity, rate of growth and sexual maturity. Furthermore, when average groups of normal people are considered, there are no exceptions to the laws of physiology. The nutritional needs of similar individuals living in broadly comparable environments are the same wherever in the globe they happen to be and whatever type of diet they may happen to be accustomed to eat. For example, in 1946 a study was made of the state of well-being of the Otomi Indians living in the Mezquital Valley in Mexico. The health of these Indians was found to be quite satisfactory, yet they were found to be eating very few of the foods, such as meat, dairy produce, fruit and vegetables, often considered in industrialised countries to be necessary for a good diet. Instead they made their meals from tortillas and from a variety of exotic local plants—including such things as pigweed, sorrel, wild mustard flowers, sow-thistle and cactus fruit. Instead of milk, they drank pulque, an intoxicating beverage prepared from the juice of the century plant. Nevertheless, when the component items of this diet were flown to the Massachusetts Institute of Technology and analysed, it was found to provide a better nutritional balance than was present in the diet of a group of United States town-dwellers surveyed at the same time.

Nutrition, although it deals with food and meals and health

2

and growth is based on two more fundamental sciences, chemistry and physiology. The reason why a certain mixture of foods, whether it be roast beef, Yorkshire pudding, potatoes, cabbage and a pint of beer or, on the other hand, tortillas, wild mustard flowers and cactus fruit, provides a nourishing diet whereas another mixture does not depend on the chemical components of the two mixtures.

LIFE IS A CHEMICAL PROCESS

It was as long ago as 1790 that the French scientist, Antoine Lavoisier, first demonstrated that life was a *chemical* process. In broad terms what he discovered was that when a material such as sugar, for example, is burned the energy released in the heat of combustion is chemical energy. Sugar is composed of carbon and hydrogen and some oxygen as well. The chemical reaction represented by burning is the combination of the carbon and the hydrogen with oxygen from the atmosphere. When these elements react, carbon dioxide gas (CO_2) and hydrogen oxide (H_2O, which is water) are formed. The energy of burning can be used either as heat, or to do work in a steam engine or motor car, or to produce electricity in a dynamo which can in its turn be used for heat or work or light. Lavoisier carried out experiments in which he showed that, for both men and animals, the energy of life could be accounted for by the known chemical energy of combusted sugar according to the known amount of oxygen used up and the known amount of carbon dioxide breathed out.

In the time that has elapsed since Lavoisier's day the basic correctness of his conclusion has been completely vindicated and we now know that life is indeed a chemical process. It is true that the chemical processes of life are more complicated than those which occur in a chemical laboratory or in a factory but they are chemical nevertheless and have been elucidated in considerable detail.

3

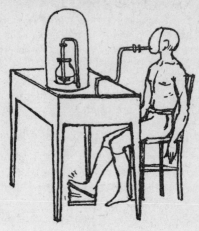

FIGURE 1.

Lavoisier's arrangement for measuring usage of oxygen and production of carbon dioxide varying with the amount of work the man did by pumping with his foot.

The Chemistry of Physical Energy

The main fuel from which physical energy is derived is *glucose*. There is no need to buy it from a chemist's shop because, as is described in Chapter 2, it is readily obtained from food. Much of human energy comes from the combustion of glucose as it combines chemically with the oxygen of the air. The important difference between the chemical mechanism of life and the chemical processes of non-life are clearly shown by the fact that whereas a pinch of glucose in contact with air in the laboratory would remain quite inert, unless it were heated up to the point at which it would burn, the same amount of glucose in a muscle could combine with oxygen and release energy with steady vigour at the quite moderate temperature of the blood.

The subtle and remarkable nature of life chemistry is that in living cells there is a series of "shoe-horn" compounds so constructed as to be able to bring about the release of chemical energy from the fuels, such as glucose, supplied by foodstuffs. But whereas in a kitchen or workshop, the energy release would be brought about by the rough and ready method of burning at high temperature, in a living creature the ultimate chemical release of energy is achieved gradually in a series of reactions which proceed step by step. And each step is brought about by means of a special "shoe-horn" compound which is so constructed as to fit into the partly combusted fuel at each particular stage. These "shoe-horn" substances are known in general chemistry as *catalysts*. In the chemistry of living cells they are called *enzymes*. They are of particular interest in nutrition because the active part of certain enzymes is made up of the specially important components of food called *vitamins*.

The Chemical Structure of Living Tissues

All living things, whether they are plants or animals, are composed of a complex honeycomb structure mainly made up of the chemical element, carbon. The elastic nature of human and animal muscles is due to the fact that interlocked as an essential part of the carbon mesh there is a proportion of atoms of the element, nitrogen, as well. Muscle, in fact, is built up of twenty or thirty compound units, chemically composed of carbon, nitrogen and hydrogen with some oxygen and sulphur here and there. These units are combined together in a similar manner to the combination of "monomer" units in a plastics factory to make such "polymers" as polythene, nylon or terylene. In fact, the tissues of flesh are, in chemical terms, natural polymers.

Most of the living tissues of the body are in a state of constant change. Consequently, there is a need for a continuous supply of new structural material, quite apart from the extra supplies required by children, young people and expectant mothers where new tissue is being grown. A human being possesses limited abilities in his body to carry out the chemical synthesis of structural material, some of the components required need to be obtained ready made in food. This, then, brings us to the need to consider the chemistry of food. Before doing so, however, it will be useful to make three definitions.

DEFINITIONS

1. **Nutrition** is the science that deals with the study of all the processes concerned in the growth, maintenance and repair of the living body which are connected in a fairly direct way with the nutrients supplied by food.

2. **Life,** by which living creatures are distinguished from those which are inanimate or non-living, is a chemical process in which an organism obtains from food the energy for its activity and the materials for its growth, maintenance and reproduction.

3. **Food** is anything, either solid or liquid, that has a chemical composition which enables it, when swallowed, to do one or more of three things:

(a) provide the body with material from which it can produce heat, work or other forms of energy.

(b) provide material to allow growth, maintenance, repair or reproduction to proceed.

(c) supply substances which normally regulate the production of energy or the process of growth, repair or reproduction.

The number of different substances that can be used for food is very large, yet every one of these substances can only qualify to rank as a food, according to the definition given above, if it is itself made up of one or more special components, called *nutrients*.

CATEGORIES OF NUTRIENTS OF WHICH FOODS ARE COMPOSED

Nutrient category	Principal function
1. Carbohydrates	Fuel for bodily activity; may also be converted into stored fat.
2. Fats	Concentrated source of energy; may also themselves be stored as body fat.
3. Proteins	Provide energy; also material for growth and repair; sometimes converted into stored fat.
4. Mineral substances	Provide special material for growth; for regulation of body processes; for repair and maintenance.
5. Vitamins	Regulate vital processes; help to catalyse certain chemical mechanisms in the body.

We shall be discussing the nature and function of these nutrients of which foods are composed in more detail in later chapters. So far as the chemistry of food as a whole is concerned, there are certain basic facts that it is useful to understand.

1. The chemical composition of foods must be such that the nutrients of which they are composed are able to dissolve in the liquid of the digestive tract and thence to penetrate through the tract into the bloodstream by which it is surrounded.

2. If the nutrients in the food eaten cannot at once penetrate the lining of the digestive tract, their chemical composition must be such that they are capable of being split by the digestive enzymes into smaller parts which are then able to pass into the bloodstream.

3. The components of food which reach the blood circulation must be of an appropriate chemical composition so that they can take part in the life chemistry of the living cells of the body.

Salt is a food because it provides elements necessary for the balance and regulation of physiological processes. It is quickly dissolved as soon as it is taken into the mouth and rapidly passes into the bloodstream. It, therefore, illustrates the first chemical principle set out above. Meat is also a food but protein which is one of its most important constituents is not at once soluble. It is, however, readily broken down by *pepsin*, an enzyme found in the stomach, into smaller soluble fractions which are able to pass through the lining of the gut. Thus it illustrates the second principle.

The third chemical principle, that, even when they are absorbed, food components must be useful to the body, can be illustrated by reference to saccharine. This purely artificial sweetening agent is readily dissolved and passed into the bloodstream. But it does not do any good when it gets there. The cells of the body can make no use of it and its chemistry, therefore, prevents our accepting it as being a food.

The chemistry of life and the nature of the chemical substances that play a part in it constitutes the science of biochemistry. This subject is dealt with in a separate book.*

PHYSIOLOGY

Physiology is the science which deals with the way in which living beings function. The study of human nutrition, besides depending in part on chemistry, must also be related to the principles of physiology. It is, for example, common knowledge, that the temperature of the human body must be maintained at or about 98·4°F., or 37°C., if it is to function harmoniously. Similarly, the blood must always be just slightly alkaline. If it becomes to any material degree acid, again the co-operative functioning of all the systems which compose an individual man is brought to a standstill. Indeed, one of

* *Teach Yourself Biochemistry* by P. H. Jellinck.

the cardinal principles of human physiology is that the constancy of the interior environment must be maintained at all times. Thus, although sugar is a food which can play an important part in the nourishment of the body and although the chemistry of sugar makes it readily soluble and easily absorbed through the digestive tract into the bloodstream, there is a physiological mechanism which almost instantly removes the sugar from the blood so that it will not contravene the cardinal principle and upset the constancy of the internal environment of the body. When people suffer from the disease diabetes, their physiological mechanism fails and the amount of sugar in their blood increases when they eat sugary foods. Unless something is done about it they may suffer from diabetic coma which could kill them.

Physiology deals with the entire mechanism of the body. It is concerned with the pumping of blood by the heart, the maintenance of body temperature and the function of the sweat glands by which it may be controlled, respiration, seeing, hearing, the nervous system, the movement and operation of the digestive system, and indeed with all the variety of organisations which combine to make up a living person. It is not the purpose of this book to attempt to describe the physiology of man but, nevertheless, a nutritionist can never forget that the facts with which he deals are only valid within the limits set by physiological possibilities.

GOOD NUTRITION

A satisfactory diet which is capable of supporting the individual who eats it in a state of good nutrition must be composed of a variety of foods which together contain the right amounts of all the various nutrients needed by the body. At the same time, the diet must provide just the right amount of fuel to allow the person eating it to execute his or her physical work. That is to say, it must provide enough to eat.

MALNUTRITION AND UNDERNUTRITION

The different nutrients supplying the needs of the body from each of the five categories, listed on page 7, comprise an extensive list. If there is a wrong proportion of one or other of these nutrients for a longer time than the body can support, a condition of *malnutrition* will occur.

If the total amount of nutrients provided by a diet is insufficient, a state of *undernutrition* will develop. The most extreme form of undernutrition is *starvation* but the way in which starvation develops will be affected by the particular way in which the diet is most grossly inadequate. In many instances it may not be possible to draw a sharp line between malnutrition and undernutrition.

Malnutrition may be caused by a wrong balance of nutrients as well as by simple inadequacy of one or other of them. Stunting in the growth of children due to lack of protein, or cracking and ulceration of the lips, due to a shortage of vitamins, may be as appropriately described as malnutrition as may excessive fatness due to over-eating.

THE MULTIPLE FUNCTION OF FOODS

People sometimes ask, "do potatoes make you fat?" or "does spinach supply you with iron?" or even such general questions as, "will beef steak make you strong?" It is important to remember that the adequacy of a diet depends on the total content of nutrients provided by the entire mixture of foods eaten. Under the category of "food" must also be included drink, where such drink supplies nutrients. The answer to the sort of questions given above is that they cannot be answered at all without further knowledge about the rest of the diet. Even when this further information is available, it is hard to answer such questions in terms of foods;

the answers are better given in terms of nutrients. When this is done, the multiple function of food becomes apparent, for example potatoes provide *Calories* and too many calories make people fat. But potatoes also contain *vitamin C* and rank, therefore, as a "protective" food. They also supply *protein* in quite useful, if small, quantities and could therefore be argued to contribute to muscular growth and hence to strength. And this kind of answer would apply to almost all such questions.

THINGS CONSUMED THAT ARE NOT FOODS

The biochemistry of life takes place in *water*. The living cells in the organs and muscles depend on a constant watery environment being maintained within them. The deprivation which would first bring human life to a stop is lack of oxygen; the second is lack of water. I am making the arbitrary decision not to include either water or air within the definition of food.

Certain other materials taken into the body are not foods either. Reference has already been made to the flavouring agent, saccharine, which is absorbed but not utilised by the body. Liquid paraffin, sometimes used as a laxative, is hardly absorbed at all and passes through the gut without becoming available to the body. Bran, also used as a laxative, is also hardly absorbed at all and, consequently, it also is not a food. Salt is absorbed and performs a useful function; therefore it is a food. Pepper is not. Tea exerts an effect on the nervous system but is not a normal regulatory substance. It is a drug, not a food. On the other hand, the milk and sugar taken with tea *are* foods. Alcohol is also a drug but it does provide energy and it must, therefore, be accepted as falling within the definition of food.

CHAPTER TWO

CARBOHYDRATES

As we have seen from the last chapter, the living body is a chemical engine and because it is an engine it must, like the engine of a motor car, be constantly supplied with fuel to keep it going. Such fuel needs to be provided by the food we eat, and when it is supplied to the body it is "combusted" with the oxygen of the air we breathe. The result of this "combustion" is the release of the necessary energy to keep us alive.

It is important to distinguish between the energy needed to keep the living system going and what in ordinary speech we think of as *energy*. In scientific terms the laziest man alive uses up energy to breathe, to keep his heart beating and his muscles in tension one against the other whether or not he ever gets his work at the office done or his letters answered. What we call an "energetic" person, someone "full of energy", may not necessarily expend more calorific energy, using the term in its proper technical sense, than the idle, ineffective individual.

The special qualities of a vigorous person are derived from qualities of mind and character far more often than from the availability of dietary fuel. Because a food, glucose for example, provides the body with energy it does not follow that a person eating it will become "energetic". *Carbohydrate* is the major component of most ordinary diets and is the nutrient component of food from which most of the bodily energy is obtained.

12

THE DIFFERENT TYPES OF CARBOHYDRATE

Carbohydrates are the chemical compounds which are synthesised by plants and which are the form in which plants store their own supplies of fuel. The original synthesis occurs in the green leaves through the action of the sunlight which, basically, is the energy upon which we and all other higher forms of life depend. The first type of carbohydrate is soluble in plant sap. These initial kinds of carbohydrate are called *sugars*. Later, a kind of chemical coagulation occurs and the sugars condense in the special storage organs of the plant in the form of *starches*. Subsequently, further condensation is possible and *cellulose,* the main component of plant fibres and wood, may be formed.

1. Sugars

(i) *Glucose* is in chemical composition one of the simple sugars. It occurs in certain foods, notably onions, unripe potatoes and sweet-corn. It is, in fact, one of the first of the sugars to be produced in leaves. The sweetish taste of a stalk of grass is partly derived from glucose. Glucose occurs in the blood of man and animals and is the form in which fuel is transported within the body. The presence of glucose as such in foods is, however, of little direct interest in nutrition because more complex carbohydrates, and particularly starch, are readily broken down into glucose in the course of digestion. Probably the only occasion when glucose itself is of importance as a food is when a marathon runner in the last stages of exhaustion needs an immediate supply of energy to maintain maximum effort after a prolonged period at full stretch. Even then a lump of sugar would be equally effective. Another occasion when pre-formed glucose may be useful is for an ill or convalescent person who is unable to eat a proper diet and for whom a solution of sugar would be too sweet.

(ii) *Fructose* is also a simple sugar. It is similar in composition to glucose and, in fact, glucose becomes converted into fructose during the process of the release of energy in the body. Fructose can be prepared from cane sugar of which, chemically, it forms a part. It occurs naturally in plant juices, in grapes and other fruit and it is a major component of honey.

(iii) *Sucrose* is the scientific name [for what is commonly called "sugar". Chemically it consists of a combination of glucose and fructose. It occurs naturally in sugar-beet and sugar-cane, which is a member of the grass family. It is also present in sweet fruits and in roots such as carrots. The belief that cane sugar is different in some way from beet sugar is a fallacy; both are identical and consist of almost completely pure sucrose. The difference between the different grades of sugar, for example, brown sugar, Demarara sugar, icing sugar, castor sugar, lump sugar and so on is due either to the method of refining or to the size of crystals prepared in the sugar factory.

(iv) *Lactose* is the sugar which occurs naturally in both human and cow's milk. Chemically it is somewhat similar to sucrose. It also is a combination of two units of simple sugar but whereas sucrose is composed of a combination of glucose and fructose, lactose is made up of glucose combined with a sugar called *galactose*. Lactose is less sweet than sucrose.

(v) *Maltose* is derived from malt and is consequently the principal sugar in malt extract. It is produced naturally from starch when grain germinates. That is to say, when a dormant seed of barley starts to grow, the fuel stored within it in the form of granules of starch is broken up into a soluble form available to the plant. This available sugar is maltose. Chemically maltose, like sucrose and lactose, is composed also of two units of simple sugar but this time they are two glucose units combined together.

2. Starches

A grain of wheat consists fundamentally of a comparatively small, dormant embryo. This is the germ from which the new plant would develop if the grain were planted in soil and watered. This embryo is separated from the larger part of the grain by a flat plate of plant tissue called the scutellum (Latin for "shield"). Beyond the scutellum is a large store of food intended for the maintenance of the young plant during its early growing period until its leaves have grown and it is able to feed itself by catching the sunlight and the carbon dioxide gas from the atmosphere. The stored food in the grain, protected by the surrounding layers of bran and outer coatings, is composed of granules of starch. It is this starch which forms by far the largest proportion of the carbohydrates we use for food.

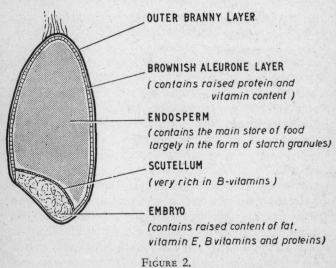

OUTER BRANNY LAYER

BROWNISH ALEURONE LAYER
(contains raised protein and
vitamin content)

ENDOSPERM
(contains the main store of food
largely in the form of starch granules)

SCUTELLUM
(very rich in B-vitamins)

EMBRYO
(contains raised content of fat,
vitamin E, B vitamins and proteins)

FIGURE 2.

A grain of wheat.

Starch is present in many other foods besides wheat and the flour which is, in fact, the main starch store of the grain. More than half the dry substance of potatoes is also made up of starch; unripe apples and bananas also contain starch but this starch changes into sugars as the fruits ripen.

Chemically, starch is composed of complex chains; the links of which are made up of glucose sugar units. Some of these chains are quite long and are made up of numerous units of glucose linked end to end, other chains are branched. All these large complex molecules of starch occur in potatoes, flour and in other cereals such as rice, oats and maize enclosed in granules. These granules can easily be seen with a microscope and differ in appearance from each other depending on the source from which they are derived. Starch granules are designed to preserve the starch during the time the various cereal grains are dormant. They are, therefore, quite resistant to digestion. This is the reason why flour, potatoes and other starch-containing foods cannot readily be eaten raw. When such foods are heated, the starch granules swell and eventually burst. The starch is then released in a digestible state.

3. Glycogen

Glycogen is similar in composition to starch and to some extent serves the same purpose in animal cells that starch performs in plant cells. That is to say it is combined stored fuel. It is laid down in the liver and muscles. After a big meal of carbohydrate the stores of glycogen in the animal body increase. On the other hand, after hard spells of muscular effort, the stored supplies of glycogen may become almost exhausted. Glycogen occurs in liver but only very small amounts are present in most meat since it is quickly broken down into glucose after the death of the animal. There are, however, two types of meat from animals which are capable of prolonged feats of muscular endurance which contain significant amounts of glycogen. These are horse meat and oysters.

4. Cellulose

As we have already seen, sugars are synthesised by the green leaves of plants under the action of sunlight. Some plants retain the sugars in their tissues. Notable among these are sugar-cane and sugar-beet. Other plants link the sugar units together chemically and store the resulting compound as starch which later we make use of as food by neglecting all the parts of the plant other than the organ in which the starch is laid down. In cereals this is the grain and in potatoes it is the tuber. But plants may combine sugar units in a different way to produce the structural framework of their cells or to give stiffness and strength to their stalks. This complex compound is cellulose.

The fibrous parts of vegetables contain cellulose and it is also a major component of straw and wood. The way in which the sugar units are chemically combined in cellulose is

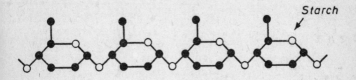

Starch

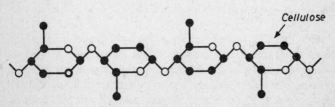

Cellulose

FIGURE 3.

A comparison of the chemical configuration of starch and of cellulose.

different from the way in which they are combined in starch, as is shown in Figure 3. The digestive *enzymes* in the human digestive tract are unable to unlink the sugar in cellulose although it can deal with the linkage in starch. Cellulose is, therefore, almost completely unavailable to the body as food. Although human beings cannot make use of cellulose as food, ruminating cattle can do so through the action of the micro-organisms on their rumen. Certain insects, for example the death-watch beetle and wood-worm sometimes found in old furniture, can, however, obtain energy from cellulose.

5. Hemi-cellulose

Hemi-cellulose is a compound which is midway in complexity between cellulose and starch. If cellulose in straw is subjected to mild chemical treatment it is converted into hemi-cellulose which is partially available to cattle as food. Hemi-cellulose occurs naturally in certain human foods. Among these are beans of the kind that are commonly eaten baked. Hemi-cellulose is only digestible to a negligible degree but it is partially attacked by micro-organisms in the human gut. This is the reason why baked beans are sometimes found to cause flatulence.

6. Pectin

Pectin is a complex carbohydrate present in apples and other fruit and in roots such as turnips. It has the property of forming stiff jellies and is, therefore, useful in making jam set. Pectin, like hemi-cellulose, is of no direct value as an energy-producing food for man. Certain modern research experiments suggest, however, that it may be of some significance in maintaining the health of the circulatory system. This suggestion, however, still needs to be confirmed.

FOODS WHICH CONTRIBUTE
CARBOHYDRATE TO THE DIET

The carbohydrates that are absorbed by the body are the *sugars* and *starches*. Both these kinds of carbohydrates serve the same purpose which is to provide energy. If the amount of energy is more than that required, the excess of carbohydrate may be converted into body fat. In comparing the contribution of carbohydrate made by different foods, it is convenient to set down the total amount of carbohydrate available to the body rather than the separate proportions of sugars and starch. This has been done in the list below and in the tables at the end of the book.

There are very few foods which contain only one single nutrient. Sugar is one of these; it consists solely of carbohydrate, namely, sucrose. Cooking fats and oils are foods which are also composed of a single nutrient, in this instance, fat. But most foods are mixtures. For example bread is predominantly a source of carbohydrate but it also contributes protein; potatoes are carbohydrate foods, but they also contain protein and vitamin C—and both these foods possess other constituents as will be discussed later.

METRIC UNITS

In science, the metric units of weight are generally used. Because nutrition deals with food, it has been found convenient to apply the metric weights of the various nutrients, that is protein, carbohydrate, fat, minerals and vitamins, to the weights commonly used by British housewives and caterers. Thus, it will be seen in the list below that the amounts of carbohydrate present in different foods are expressed as so many *grams* per *ounce* (abbreviated to " g. per oz.").

19

A gram (also spelled "gramme") is a unit of weight.

$$28 \cdot 36 \text{ g.} = 1 \text{ oz.}$$
$$\text{or } 100 \text{ g.} = 3\tfrac{1}{2} \text{ oz.}$$

TABLE 1

THE AVAILABLE CARBOHYDRATE CONTENT OF COMMON FOODS

(g. per oz. of edible portion)

Jams and preserves		*Fruit*	
Sugar	27·0	Raisins	16·5
Syrup	20·2	Dates	16·3
Jam	17·6	Currants	16·0
		Banana	4·9
Cereals		Grapes	4·1
Flour, white	21·2	Apples	3·0
„ wholemeal	17·4	Pineapple	3·0
Bread, white	15·6	Oranges	2·2
„ wholemeal	11·2		
Rice	22·2	*Dairy produce*	
Oatmeal	18·6	Sweetened condensed	
		milk	14·1
Vegetables		Evaporated milk	2·7
Potatoes	4·6	Whole milk (fresh)	1·2
Beans (baked)	4·5	Eggs	0·3
Parsnips	2·9	Cheese	nil
Peas (green)	2·7		
Beetroot	2·3	*Meat and fish*	
Cabbage	1·4	Liver (ox)	1·4
Spinach	0·7	Meat	nil
		Fish	nil

CHAPTER THREE

FATS

THE substances that we know as "fats", whether they are derived from pigs as pork fat or lard, from cattle as beef fat, dripping or butter fat, or from sheep as suet or mutton fat, all belong to the same category of chemical compounds, namely, *the fats*. Vegetable oils—olive oil, maize oil, peanut oil or cocoa butter—and fish oils as well are also all *fats*. Whether a particular fat is liquid at room temperature, and is consequently known in common speech as an oil, is of little significance nutritionally although it may be of some importance in cooking. This is merely a matter of temperature. When cooking fat is heated in a frying-pan it becomes a liquid oil; if coconut oil is kept in a cold larder it solidifies into a solid fat.

Of all the components of diet, fat is the most concentrated source of energy. Although starch is the most common energy-storage substance in cereals and other botanical species, some plants can also store energy in the even more compact form of fat. When seeds such as cotton-seed or linseed ripen, the amount of starch in them falls and the amount of fat rises. Oil seeds, such as these, are among the most important sources of fat for human consumption in the form of margarine and other compound fats or directly as cooking fats.

Animals, like plants, can also convert excess carbohydrate into fat. If an individual eats more carbohydrate than he needs for the muscular work of the day, part of the excess will be stored in the body as fat. In just the same way, pigs and sheep and cattle—or, for that matter, geese—which are fed carbohydrate in excess of their current needs will become fat. Animal fat may be formed from fat derived from the diet as well as from carbohydrate. Although the food fat will be partly changed by the animal eating it, it may not be changed completely. Consequently, if a pig is given large amounts of cod-liver oil in its feed, its own fat will take on a fishy taste when it in its turn comes to be eaten by us.

THE CHEMICAL COMPOSITION OF FATS

The chemical nature of fats affects the way they behave in cooking as well as the way they behave as food. Chemically, fats are made up of three units of *fatty acid* combined together by each being attached to a single unit of *glycerol*. (Glycerol is a substance that is often called "glycerine" in common speech.) The most distinctive property of fats of all sorts is that they do not mix with water. The saying about oil and water not mixing is, indeed, a scientific observation. But although the chemical combination of three fatty acids and one glycerol (that is to say, *fat*) will not mix with water, the three parts separated will.

In a laboratory, a single unit of fat can be split into its component parts by treatment with caustic soda or some other alkali. The fatty acids are converted into *soaps* and the released glycerol goes free. The process of treating fat in this way is, in fact, called *saponification*, that is soap formation. The same process occurs during the course of digestion.

All fats and oils, that are useful to the body as food, are capable of being saponified; mineral oils such as liquid paraffin or vaseline cannot be saponified. They are therefore unavailable to the body and cannot consequently be included within the definition of food at all.

Although fatty acids all belong to the same chemical class, they differ one from another. The differences between different fats and different oils is due to the different fatty acid

TABLE 2

THE PRINCIPAL SOURCES OF FAT IN THE BRITISH DIET

	%
Fats (butter, margarine, cooking fats, etc.)	40
Meat (including bacon)	32
Dairy produce (excluding butter and eggs)	16
Cereals (bread, flour, etc.)	6
Eggs	2
Other foods	4
	100

It can be seen from Table 2 that although about two-fifths of the fat in the British diet is derived from "visible" fats such as butter, margarine and cooking fat, one-third is derived from meat and one-sixth largely from milk. This underlines the importance in nutrition in always remembering that the contribution made by any particular food to the diet as a whole depends on two factors (a) the proportion of any nutrient in the individual food and (b) the amount of that food eaten during the course of a day.

The amounts of fat in some of the foods which contribute significantly to the total fat content of the diet are shown in Table 3.

TABLE 3

THE FAT CONTENT OF SOME COMMON FOODS
(g. per oz.: average values)

Fats and oils		Dairy Produce	
Frying oil	28·4	Cream	11·9
Lard, dripping, cooking fat	28·1	Cheese, Cheddar	9·8
		Eggs	3·3
Margarine	24·2	Milk, condensed	2·6
Butter	23·4	Milk	1·0

combinations which go to make up each individual fat or oil. The chemical basis of every fatty acid is a string of linked carbon atoms. This string may, however, be of varying length. Furthermore, the linking of one carbon "bead" to the next may be simple or there may be a degree of tension. The effects of some of these differences are:

1. **Butyric acid** is a fatty acid with a short string of 4-carbon atoms. Combined as fat it gives *butter*, in which it is a major ingredient, some of its characteristic flavour. If the chemical structure of butter fat breaks down, for example, if it becomes rancid, the free butyric acid gives the smell of rancidity.

2. **Caproic acid** contains 6 carbon atoms in its chain. It is an ingredient of coconut fat and of butter fat. *Caprylic acid* contains 8 carbon atoms and *capric acid* 10 carbon atoms. These fatty acids occur in human fat and also in goat's fat (*caper* is Latin for a goat). They possess a goaty smell.

3. **Palmitic acid** and **stearic acid** are present in a great many fats but are most commonly found in *solid fats*. They contain chains of 16 and 18 carbon atoms respectively.

4. **Oleic acid**, like stearic acid, is a chain of 18 carbon atoms but this chain is not all made up of simple links, one of the links is under tension. The effect of this is to make fats containing oleic acid liquid oils at normal room temperature; whereas those containing stearic acid are solid fats.

5. **Linoleic acid, linolenic acid** and **arachidonic acid** are also 18-carbon-chain fatty acids but their chains contain two, three and four points of tension respectively. These fatty acids are found in vegetable oils but are less common than oleic acid. Their special interest in nutrition is discussed in a later paragraph.

The chemical nature of these fatty acids is shown diagrammatically in Figure 4.

Intact fat, in which the three fatty acids units remain anchored to the unit of glycerol that holds them together, will

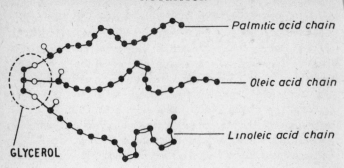

FIGURE 4.

The chemical structure of fat

not dissolve in water or mix readily with water. Fats are, however, soluble in liquids called "fat solvents" such as petrol, benzine or ether. As has already been described, a unit of fat can be *saponified* and when this is done, the two parts— the soaps and the glycerol—*can* be dissolved in water. In most natural fats, however, there are substances which occur mixed with the fat and which cannot be saponified. Some of these members of the *unsaponifiable residue* of a natural fat are of nutritional importance:

SUBSTANCES IN THE UNSAPONIFIABLE PORTION OF FATS

1. *Vitamins* A, D, E and K which, in appropriate amounts, are nutritionally useful.

2. *Cholesterol* which, in excess, may be harmful.

"HARDENED" FATS

Fats as such all possess about the same nutritional value; that is to say, whether a fat is solid at room temperature, like mutton fat or lard, or liquid, like olive oil or peanut oil, it

nevertheless serves as an equally concentrated source energy to the body. In most northern industrial count however, the fats most commonly favoured in cooking solids and fats used as spreads, whether butter or marg are expected to be solid too. In commerce, however, the readily available fats are often liquids such as peanu cottonseed oil or whale oil. Consequently, manufac producing cooking fat or margarine take steps to "ha the oils which they use as their ingredients.

As a general rule, liquid oils contain a higher proport *unsaturated* fatty acids than solid fats. The unsaturate acids are those such as *oleic acid, linoleic acid, arachidonic a* some others that are composed of carbon chains some links of which are under tension, as has already be cribed. When fats are "hardened", a process of *hydro* is used. The fats are treated with hydrogen in such a v the strained carbon linkages are relaxed. By this oleic acid, for example, becomes converted into stea and the other *unsaturated* acids become progressively By carrying out this process of *hydrogenation* to a great degree, a manufacturer starting with a liquid oil can a fat as hard or as soft as he wishes. The possible effe process on the nutritional value of the fat is discu later paragraph.

FOODS PROVIDING FAT IN THE DI

Fat in the diet can be considered as falling into gories: "visible" fat—that is to say, fats such margarine, lard or cooking oil, which are added to recognisable and measurable form—and "invi which is contributed by meat, fish, cheese, and o The principal sources of the total "visible" and ' fat in the British diet are shown in Table 2.

Meat

Bacon	12·8
Pork	11·4
Mutton, average	8·8
Beef, average	8·0
Beef, corned	4·5
Liver	1·7
Veal	1·0

Fish

Sardine	6·8
Kipper	4·5
Herring	3·3
Salmon	2·8
Cod, white fish	0·3

Cereals

Oatmeal	2·5
Wholemeal bread	0·6
Barley	0·5
Rice	0·3
White bread	0·2

Fruit

All sorts	Nil

Vegetables

Potatoes	
Green vegetables	Nil
Peas and beans	

The following points should be noted about fat in foods:

1. Cooking fat and frying oil are almost 100% fats. They contain no water so that their contribution of energy is higher than that of all other foods.

2. Butter and margarine, although conventionally thought of as fats, contain only 84 to 89% of fat and a proportion of water and salt as well.

3. Meat makes an important contribution of fat to the diet. It must always be remembered, however, in considering the nutritional value of a diet, that—as is well known domestically —the fat content of one piece of meat may vary very widely from another.

4. Fish fall into two categories: *fat fish*, including herring, mackerel, salmon, sardine, pilchard and eel contribute quite substantial amounts of fat. The exact proportion of fat in them is, however, affected to some extent by the time of year and the state of their breeding cycle. *White fish*, such as cod, whiting, haddock and sole contain very little fat.

THE SPECIAL NUTRITIONAL AND DIETETIC CHARACTERISTICS OF FAT

1. **Energy value.** As is discussed in more detail in Chapter 5, fats are the richest dietary sources of energy available to the body. Fats are also very *useful in cooking*. It follows, therefore, that when foods are cooked in fat their energy value is much increased. For example, "chips" have three times the energy value of boiled potatoes, pastry has more than twice the energy value of bread, and fried onions have about fourteen times more energy value than raw onion. This means that although fat is valuable to people who expend energy on heavy muscular labour, it can imperceptibly supply an excess to people who lead a sedentary life.

2. **Satiety value.** Fat delays the passage of food through the stomach and in consequence it gives a more prolonged feeling of satisfaction than other nutrients. To use a vernacular expression, foods containing an appreciable proportion of fat "stay with you" longer than those that do not.

3. **Heart disease.** Some nutritionists and research workers but not all, believe that the alarming increase in coronary heart disease, particularly among middle-aged and older men, is partly due to the deposition of *cholesterol* in their arteries. The concentration of cholesterol in the blood tends to rise when a diet rich in certain fats is eaten, and when the person eating the diet takes too little exercise. The advice is therefore being given that an excessive diet should be avoided (excess being indicated by overweight) and that particularly the types of fat that have been shown most markedly to increase the blood cholesterol level should be replaced by fats that do not. Present state of knowledge suggests that *saturated fatty acids* cause the cholesterol level to rise, *unsaturated fatty acids with one point of tension* (e.g. oleic acid) have little effect, while *unsaturated fatty acids with more than one point of tension* (e.g.

linoleic, linolenic and arachidonic acids) reduce the concentration of cholesterol in the blood. Fats, the component fatty acids of which exert these three effects, are listed in Table 4. The same effect is also produced by eating too much sugar and taking too little exercise.

TABLE 4

THE EFFECT OF DIFFERENT FATS ON CHOLESTEROL IN BLOOD

Fats that raise the cholesterol level	Fats that have little effect on cholesterol level	Fats that lower the cholesterol level
Butter	Peanut oil (arachis)	Maize oil (corn oil)
Margarine	Olive oil	Cottonseed oil
Beef fat		Sunflower seed oil
Mutton fat		Soya bean oil
Cooking fat		Sesame oil
Lard		Safflower oil
Coconut oil		Fish oils

CHAPTER FOUR

PROTEIN

CARBOHYDRATES and fats are composed of carbon, hydrogen and oxygen. They serve the body as a fuel to produce energy and when they do so they become combusted with the inhaled oxygen of the air by a complex sequence of interlinked reactions, until as carbon dioxide gas (CO_2) and water (H_2O) they are finally excreted in the breath. It is from this chain of chemical reactions that the energy of life is fundamentally derived.

Protein, like carbohydrate and fat, also contains carbon and hydrogen and these too are combusted *to yield energy for the body*. But, besides being built up of a structure of carbon, protein is composed of unit sections, called *amino acids*, and these amino acids also contain *nitrogen* as an essential part of their composition.

Protein is the real stuff of the living body. It is, in fact, an essential constituent of the living cells of all higher creatures, plants as well as animals. Consequently, an abundance of protein is necessary for *growth*. It follows, therefore, that protein is a nutrient of particular importance to *expectant mothers, infants, children* and *adolescents* and also following injury and disease when damaged body tissues have to be made good.

Protein is also an essential nutrient in the diet of ordinary adults. The protein in the body of a grown man or woman does not stay still. It is continuously being broken down and built up again and in the course of this process a small proportion is continuously being lost. This loss—sometimes, and not very appropriately, called "wear and tear"—can only be made good by enough of the right kind of protein. The energy value of the diet can be supplied indifferently by carbohydrate or by fat or by protein, but the requirements for the construction of new living cells in growing children and for the maintenance of the existing living cells of adults can only be met by adequate amounts of protein.

THE SOURCES OF PROTEIN IN THE DIET

There are two sources of protein for nutrition, (1) from animal foods and (2) from the parts of plants of which their living cells are composed.

Animal protein is derived from:
Meat. Poultry and *game. Fish* and *shell fish.*
Milk and such *milk products* as cheese, dried milk and evaporated milk but *not* from butter or cream.

Vegetable protein is derived from:
Peas and beans which, as seeds, form a specially rich store.
Nuts which are also seeds of the plants that bear them.
Cereals contain protein but particularly in the embryo and certain of the seed coats, consequently flour contains progressively less protein the more carefully it is separated from the embryo and outer coats during the course of milling.
Green leafy vegetables contribute protein but the amount may be limited because of their high water content.
Potatoes also provide some protein but, again, the amount may be small because they too are quite watery and besides contain a substantial amount of starch.
Root vegetables being mostly water, contribute little protein to the diet.

Table 5 shows the amount of protein in a number of the more important foods usually found in a Western diet.

TABLE 5

THE PROTEIN CONTENT OF CERTAIN FOODS
(g. per oz. of edible portion)

Meat

Beef corned	7·1
Veal	5·3
Liver	4·8
Kidney	4·5
Beef	4·0–5·2
Mutton	3·8
Pork	3·4
Bacon	3·1

Fish

Salmon	5·7
Sardine	5·7
Kipper	5·4
Herring	4·5
Cod and other white fish	4·5

Dairy produce

Dried egg	13·0
Dried skim milk	10·2
Cheese	7·1
Milk, evaporated	2·0
Milk, fresh	0·9

Cereals

Flour, wholemeal	3·9
Oatmeal	3·4
Bread, wholemeal	3·1
Bread, white	2·3
Barley	2·2
Rice	1·8

Vegetables

Peas, dried	7·0
Lentils, dried	6·8
Beans, haricot	6·1
Peas, green	1·6
Spinach	0·8
Cauliflower	0·7
Potatoes	0·6
Onion	0·3
Carrot	0·2
Turnip	0·2

Nuts

Peanut	8·0
Almonds	5·1

The table above shows that such foods as dried egg and peanuts are richest in protein. But again, as with fat, it is important to remember that the significance of any article to nutrition depends upon the amount of it that is eaten as well as the percentage of any particular nutrient there may be in that special article. Table 6 shows the food from which protein was actually obtained in the British diet in Britain as a whole.

TABLE 6

THE SOURCES OF PROTEIN IN THE NATIONAL DIET

	%
Bread, flour, etc.	40
Dairy produce	20
Meat	17
Fish, poultry	6
Potatoes	6
Eggs	4
Other foods	7
	100

THE CHEMISTRY OF PROTEIN

Proteins are *polymers*, that is to say, like such artificial polymers as polythene and perspex, or nylon, terylene or PVC (poly-vinyl-chloride), they are made up of a series of chemical unit parts, which are called *monomers*, arranged in such an order as to give each protein its particular property. Beef is different from chicken, in just the same way as nylon is different from terylene, because the unit monomers are different and are put together differently.

The monomer units of which proteins are composed are called *amino acids*. Each consists of a carbon skeleton of varying shape and size but each always contains as well as part of its essential structure an atom of *nitrogen*.

The use of protein as a source of energy. Protein can be readily combusted to produce energy for the body. When this occurs the carbon and hydrogen in the amino acids eventually become burned to carbon dioxide (CO_2) and water (H_2O) which are expired in the breath. The nitrogen is excreted by the kidneys and passes out of the body in the urine as a compound called "urea".

The use of protein as structural building material. The essential and peculiar function of protein as a nutrient is to serve as a source of structural material for the tissues of the body. Protein which is eaten as food is first split up into its component amino acids. There may be more than twenty different kinds of amino acids in a particular protein and a total of several hundred amino acid units in all arranged in a characteristic pattern for each protein. A growing child disconnects all these amino acids from the different articles of his diet and then rearranges them in the correct proportions and in the right order to construct his own human protein.

Of the more than twenty *different kinds* of amino acids, the body can synthesise certain individual ones. There are, however, *ten amino acids* that the body cannot make and which must, therefore, be supplied by the diet. These are called *essential amino acids*.

The food quality of protein from different sources. Not all proteins in every foodstuff contain all ten of the essential amino acids needed for the construction of human protein within the body.

(*a*) **Vegetable proteins,** from such foods as bread, dried beans or peanuts, do not contain the essential amino acids in the relative proportion required by the body. It follows, therefore, that no matter how large a total quantity of protein is consumed, if it is all derived from such vegetable sources only, the body cannot readily complete the building-up of human protein. For this reason, vegetable proteins are sometimes referred to as *second-class proteins*.

(*b*) **Animal protein.** Most proteins from animal sources, for instance from meat, milk, eggs or fish, do contain the complete list of essential amino acids in appropriate proportions. They are, therefore, readily capable of providing the body's needs of protein. And for this reason they are often known as *first-class protein*. It does not *always* happen that *every* protein derived from an animal source is a "complete", or first-class protein. For example, gelatin, although it is an animal protein derived from meat, and forms one of the principal ingredients of gristle, hoofs, horn, etc., is deficient in at least one essential amino acid, *tryptophan*.

(*c*) **Mixed protein.** Although the amino acid make-up of vegetable proteins is lacking in one or other of the essential amino acids, they are not all deficient in the same amino acid. It follows, therefore, that a *mixture* of two or more proteins, each of which may be deficient in one or other amino acid, may contain a full supply of all. For example, a diet containing an adequate supply of cereal protein *together with* green leaf protein, will be nutritionally adequate although dependence on either one or the other source *alone* would not.

Alternatively, *the addition of a small amount of animal protein* will complete the nutritional adequacy of a diet in which the main sources of protein are cereals or other foods providing what would alone be second-class protein. The way in which proteins combine to supplement each other is shown diagrammatically in Figure 5.

PROTEIN AND MUSCULAR WORK

Many people believe that when a man is doing heavy muscular work he needs extra protein, and particularly meat. There is no scientific evidence that this is so. Careful researches have been carried out with fit young men living an active life and doing heavy work under controlled conditions. Some of these men were given large amounts of protein, some small amounts and some intermediate quantities. Provided they received the requirement of protein relative to their body weight, the efficiency with which they did their work and their fitness afterwards were not affected by whether or not they received extra protein. As we have already seen, although protein can be used by the body as fuel for the production of work, the main dietary fuels are carbohydrate—either as sugar

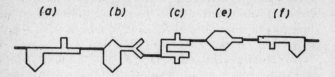

1. A portion of protein A (lacking in [d] but containing [c])

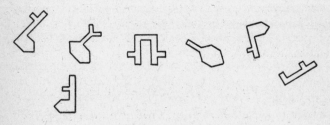

2. A portion of protein B (lacking in [c] but containing [d])

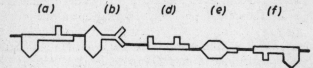

3. Amino acids split apart during digestion

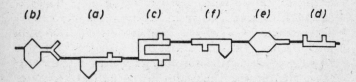

4. Human protein (incorporating both [c] and [d])

FIGURE 5.

How two incomplete proteins can supplement each other.

or starch—and fat. Meat is a useful and an attractive food for people doing heavy work. The table at the end of this book shows that besides containing protein, it also contributes quite substantial amounts of fat, which is a concentrated fuel. And the fact that meat is appetising ensures that these supplies are consumed. Excess protein of itself, however, is not of any special significance for muscular workers.

PROTEIN AND ATHLETES

At one time certain athletes used to eat large amounts of meat while they were training; but the modern tendency has been towards a simple diet of a normal type in which the amounts of food eaten are merely adjusted to provide the increased demands for energy arising from the physical exercise being undertaken. Meat is a useful food for athletes, just as it is for other muscular workers, but recent studies of a variety of athletes in training show that while some of them eat large amounts of meat there are other equally successful performers who are vegetarians and others who keep their protein consumption purposely low. It seems clear that, just as there is no scientific reason for heavy workers to consume an excess of protein, so also is there no nutritional demand for extra protein for athletes.

THE PROPERTIES OF
DIFFERENT KINDS OF PROTEIN

As we have already seen, proteins are composed *chemically* of a mosaic of *amino acid* units which may be arranged in an almost infinitely varied number of ways. Although the protein which is the major component of human skin, let us say, is composed of an amino acid pattern which is broadly similar for all human skins, there are certain differences between the patterns of different individuals. Even the patterns of the amino acids of the skins of brothers and sisters are slightly different. Consider, therefore, how different is the make-up of the protein of different types of animals and how very different is the mosaic formed by the amino acids of such diverse proteins as those from animal muscle, wheat gluten, egg albumen, hair, the protein of nuts, and casein from milk.

The chemical differences between proteins are reflected in certain differences in their physical properties. At the same time, since all proteins belong to the same *class* of substances, there are certain general similarities between all of them.

Similarities Between Different Proteins

1. When proteins are burned in a flame they all produce a somewhat similar and *characteristic smell*. A typical example is *hair*; but charred meat or egg white or gluten also has a not dissimilar smell.

2. Because proteins are natural *polymers* (i.e. "plastics") they possess physical properties which resemble those of artificial polymers. *Casein*, the protein in milk, gives cheese its characteristic rubbery consistency; it can also be hardened and, as found in some hard cheeses, can take on a remarkably tough consistency. At one time, this property of casein was used industrially for the manufacture of buttons and umbrella handles. If flour is kneaded in running water, the tough elastic material remaining when the starch has been washed out is the protein, *gluten*. Like many artificial "plastics", it can be made elastic, or hard, or rubbery.

Differences in the Properties of Individual Proteins

1. **Some proteins are soluble in water.** *Casein* in milk, *albumen* in egg, *plasma protein* in blood are examples of soluble proteins.

2. **Many proteins are not soluble in water.** Among these are some proteins in meat, in bread, peas and beans, nuts, etc.

3. **Proteins that become insoluble when they are**

heated. The egg protein, *albumen*, is one that characteristically becomes insoluble when it is heated. This is why boiling an egg for sufficiently long to heat it through makes it *hard boiled*. This change in the nature of protein when it is strongly heated is a general phenomenon called *denaturation*. But the accompanying hardening may occur to a varying degree in different proteins.

CHAPTER FIVE

FOOD, WORK, AND FATNESS

FOOD is what keeps you going. To put this statement in more scientific terms it could be said that the primary function of food is to supply energy to the living body. Life is a chemical process and the body is a chemical engine. In order that this engine shall not stop, it must constantly be supplied with fuel. We have already seen that each of the three major nutrients in food, carbohydrate, fat and protein, can provide energy. Most foods contain a mixture of these three nutrients; the energy value of a particular food is made up of the sum of the energy derived from the carbohydrate, fat and protein in that food.

CALORIES

A calorie is a unit of energy. The calorie used in nutrition (sometimes called a "Kilo calorie") is the amount of heat needed to raise the temperature of 1000 grams of water 1 degree Centigrade.*

Note : 1000 grams = approximately 2 lb. 3 oz.
       1°C = 1·8°F·

A Calorie is defined in terms of heat but this does not mean to say that the consumption of food providing, say, 100 calories—an ounce of flour, for instance—will necessarily make you hot. Heat is a form of energy. The energy value of coal is also measured in terms of calories but it is a matter of choice whether the coal is used to warm the room (that is as a source of heat), to drive a train (that is as a source of mechanical

* The unit, a Megajoule, is now coming into use in place of the calorie. 1000 calories = 4·186 MJ.

40

power), or to run a dynamo (that is as a source of electricity). Similarly, the energy value of a food measured in terms of calories *may* be used in part to warm the body, but is much more likely to be used to produce bodily power.

CALCULATING THE ENERGY VALUE OF FOOD

The energy value of any food is derived from the nutrients in it, and these nutrients when absorbed and oxidised (that is combusted) in the body produce energy as follows:

1 gram of *carbohydrate* produces 4 calories
1 gram of *protein* produces 4 calories
1 gram of *fat* produces 9 calories

It can at once be seen that the figures above give the reason why foods that contain a large amount of fat are rich in calories. Here is an example:

1 oz. of boiled cod has the following composition:

Protein	4·5 grams	= 4·5 × 4	= 18 calories
Carbohydrate	nil	—	—
Fat	0·3 grams	= 0·3 × 9	= 2·7 calories
		Total	20·7 calories

1 oz. fried cod has the following composition:

Protein	5·3 grams	= 5·3 × 4	= 21·2 calories
Carbohydrate	1·4 grams	= 1·4 × 4	= 5·6 calories
Fat	3·4 grams	= 3·4 × 9	= 30·6 calories
		Total	57·4 calories

Thus the fat in the fried fish has increased the calorie value to more than double.

THE EFFECT OF WATER
ON THE ENERGY VALUE OF FOOD

Water is not a food (in the sense in which food has been defined in this book), yet water is a major constituent of many foods. Since in nutrition we are concerned with the *quantities* of nutrients and calories provided by an *exact weight* of food, it follows that the more of the weight there is made up from water, the less nourishment and the fewer calories there will be in that weight. For instance, an ounce of turnip is composed of 93% of water. This is the main reason why it only contributes 5 calories. Again, 1 oz. of dry potato starch contains 100 calories, yet 1 oz. of potato only contains 21 calories because of that ounce 76% is made up of water.

THE CALORIE VALUE OF ALCOHOL

People drink alcohol primarily for its pharmacological effect as a sedative or, as we should now say, as a "tranquilliser". Nevertheless, it must not be overlooked that alcohol is a food that provides calories to the body.

1 gram of *alcohol* produces 7·1 calories

It can be seen that alcohol provides more energy than protein or carbohydrate and this is one reason why some drinkers get fat. Half a pint (10 oz.) of beer containing 5·4% of alcohol produces 214 calories of which 117 are derived from the alcohol.

THE ENERGY VALUE OF
SOME COMMON FOOD

In Table 7 below are listed the calorie value of a number of foods. Common knowledge will show that those commodities providing the most calories are those containing the highest proportion of fat. The precise amount can be seen by reference to the table at the end of the book. On the other hand, when considering the importance in actual practice of any single item of diet, it is not only necessary to know its calorie value *per oz.*; two other factors must also be borne in mind:

(*a*) the amount of water in the foodstuff under consideration in comparison with the amount of water it contains when it is eaten.

(*b*) the normal amount of the particular foodstuff that would be eaten at a sitting.

For example, dried peas contain 85 calories per oz. and dried beans 71 calories per oz. Peas and beans of this sort are, however, not eaten dry but only after they have been soaked. Thus a serving of baked beans, *as eaten*, provides only 25 calories per oz. Then again, bread provides 70 calories *per oz.* compared with milk with 17 or beer with 10 calories *per oz.* In this instance, however, one might eat only an ounce of bread at a particular meal, yet drink a half pint of milk, i.e. 10 oz., containing 170 calories, or a pint of beer, i.e. 20 oz. containing 200 calories.

TABLE 7

THE CALORIE VALUE OF COMMON FOODS
(Calories per oz.)

Fats		Fish	
Cooking fat, lard, etc.	253	Sardine	84
Margarine	218	Kipper	62
Butter	211	Salmon	48
		Cod, white fish, etc.	21

Cereals		Legumes	
Oatmeal	111	Dried peas	85
Flour	100	Haricot beans	71
Rice	99	Baked beans	25
Barley	97		
Bread	73	Vegetables	
		Potato	21
		Peas, fresh	17
		Cabbage	7
Meat		Turnip	5
Bacon	128	Lettuce	5
Pork	116		
Mutton (avg.)	94	Miscellaneous	
Beef (avg.)	89	Chocolate, plain	148
Liver	40	Sugar	108
Veal	31	Jam	71
		Beer, mild	10
		Fruit	
Dairy produce		Dates	68
Cheese	117	Figs, dried	58
Condensed milk	89	Banana	21
Eggs	45	Apple	12
Milk	17	Orange	10

THE UTILISATION OF
CALORIES BY THE HUMAN BODY

1. **Basal metabolism.** The basic purpose for which energy is used by the body is to maintain the machinery of life—the circulation of the blood impelled by the beating of the heart, breathing, the resting tension of the muscles, and the body temperature. This basic expenditure of energy, comparable with the petrol expended in keeping an engine ticking over, is called *basal metabolism*.

The following factors affect the number of calories needed

for basal metabolism, that is to live, warm and still, lying in bed:

(i) *Body size*

A normal man of average size is taken to require 70 calories per hour, i.e. about 1680 calories per day.

A normal woman of average size is taken to require 65 calories per hour, i.e. about 1450 calories per day.

An average man of 5 ft. 6 in. weighing 8 st. 3 lb. has a basal need of 1400 calories a day compared with an average of 1700 calories for a man 6 ft. tall weighing 11 st.

(ii) *Age*

Basal metabolism falls about 2% for each decade of age, thus between 20 and 70 years old it falls about 10%.

(iii) *Individual peculiarities*

Individual men and women may vary quite widely from the average. This may be due to temperament and build quite apart from any chemical abnormality such as malfunction of the thyroid gland.

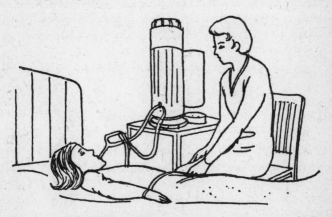

FIGURE 6.

The determination of basal metabolic rate.

2. **The everyday activities of normal life—sitting, standing, moving about, going and coming to and from work.** For people engaged in very many of the ordinary occupations of present-day industrial life, the calorie requirements of these domestic activities may form a substantial proportion of all the calories needed in addition to those for basal metabolism. The calorie requirements for different kinds of everyday activity are as follows:

	Calories per hour		Calories per hour
Sitting	15	Dusting	110
Standing	20	Walking slowly	115
Dressing and undressing	33	Walking moderately fast	215
Washing up	60	Walking upstairs	1000

Note: Thinking uses up less than 1 calorie per hour

3. **The calorie requirements of daily work.** The total daily demands for energy are made up of three components. The first two are for (*a*) basal metabolism, and (*b*) domestic activities, etc. The third set of demands arises from the muscular requirements of daily work. Types of work have been classified as light, moderate, hard and very hard depending on these demands for calorie expenditure.

(i) *Light work* (up to 75 calories an hour)

	Calories per hour		Calories per hour
Writing	20	Draftsmen	45
Typing	30	Tailoring	70
Lithographing	45	Bookbinding	70

(ii) *Moderate work* (75 to 150 calories an hour)

	Calories per hour		Calories per hour
Shoemaking	100	Electrician's work	130
Cleaning	120	Carpentering	140
Light engineering	130	Painting	150

(iii) *Hard work* (150 to 300 calories an hour)

	Calories per hour		Calories per hour
Heavy carpentry	190	Riveting	275
Polishing	170	Stonemason's work	300
Light blacksmithing	275		

(iv) *Very hard work* (over 300 calories an hour)

	Calories per hour
Coal mining	320
Heavy blacksmithing	350
Wood cutting	380

FIGURE 7.

Measuring the calorie expenditure of coal-mining.

47

THE DAILY CALORIE NEEDS OF PEOPLE FOLLOWING DIFFERENT OCCUPATIONS

The total energy expenditure during the course of a day, which must be supplied by the calories of a nutritionally adequate diet, is the sum of different amounts of calories used up by the activities of the total 24 hours. Examples of these sums are shown below:

1. MEN

(a) A tailor

		Calories
24 hours basal metabolism	(24 × 70)	1680
1 hour dressing and undressing	(1 × 33)	33
1 hour walking slowly	(1 × 115)	115
2 hours light exercise	(2 × 85)	170
4 hours sitting	(4 × 15)	60
8 hours tailoring	(8 × 80)	640
		2698

(b) A coalminer

		Calories
24 hours basal metabolism	(24 × 70)	1680
1 hour dressing and undressing	(1 × 33)	33
1 hour walking to and from work	(1 × 115)	115
8 hours leisure	(8 × 40)	320
1 hour travelling underground	(1 × 20)	20
7 hours mining	(7 × 320)	2240
		4408

2. WOMEN

(a) A typist

		Calories
24 hours basal metabolism	(24 × 60)	1440
3 hours light exercise	(3 × 80)	240
5 hours domestic life	(5 × 33)	165
8 hours typing	(8 × 30)	240
		2085

(b) *A charwoman*   *Calories*

24 hours basal metabolism	(24 × 60)	1440
1 hour walking	(1 × 200)	200
2 hours sitting	(2 × 15)	30
5 hours domestic life	(5 × 33)	165
8 hours charring	(8 × 150)	1200
		3025

APPETITE AND OBESITY

All the figures given so far for the hourly expenditure on basal metabolism, on the goings and comings of daily life, and on different kinds of work *are averages*. It must always be remembered that individual people may vary quite widely from these average values.

A simple test of whether a person is obtaining an adequate supply of calories from his daily diet is to find out whether his weight is normal for his build and age and that he is not losing weight.

Many people maintain a satisfactory weight at a steady value for a long period of years: these people are able automatically to balance their needs of calories for energy and the calories they eat as food by means of their *appetite*. Unfortunately, appetite is not always a reliable controller of calorie requirement. In certain conditions of ill-health, appetite is lost and the patient loses weight and becomes thin; more commonly, however, appetite fails to limit the amount eaten and the individual concerned gains weight and becomes too fat.

There are three principles that control obesity

1. A person whose calorie intake as food is greater than his calorie output as bodily activity will gain weight and become fat.

2. Slimming, that is loss of fat, can be achieved *only* by eating fewer calories while maintaining the same amount of bodily activity or by—

3. Continuing to eat the same diet as before but taking more exercise.

If you eat about 750 *calories fewer* than your previous standard diet you can expect to lose about 7 lb. in a month or 14 lb. in 9 weeks.

If you expend about 400 *extra calories* (by walking briskly uphill for an hour every day) you can expect to lose about 7 lb. in 2 months (provided you don't eat any more than before).

CALORIES, HOT FOOD, AND BODY TEMPERATURE

A calorie, as was stated at the beginning of this chapter, is a unit of energy that happens to be measured in terms of heat (i.e. 1 calorie = the heat to warm 1000 grams of water 1°C.). If you are cold, eating an ounce of sugar (108 calories which in *terms of heat* is enough to boil a quart of water) does not warm you. This is the same as the fact that in a car without a heater, the petrol, which is high in calories and is driving the car at 60 miles an hour, does not heat you either.

On the other hand, hot soup inside your stomach warms you just as does *hot water* in a hot-water bottle.

RECAPITULATION

The principles of nutrition that we have discussed so far are these:

1. **Food** is made up of one or more components, called *nutrients*, the chemical nature of which enable them (*a*) to provide the body with energy, (*b*) to provide the body with the components necessary for its growth and maintenance and (*c*) to regulate the body processes (these will be discussed in the next few chapters).

2. The three main *nutrients* of foods are:

   Carbohydrates, including starches, sugars and related compounds. These supply energy.

Fats which also supply energy in particularly concentrated form.

Proteins which provide energy but whose special function is to supply the component *amino acids* required for the growth and maintenance of the body cells.

3. The energy that keeps life going is measured in terms of calories. The amount of calories provided by different foods can be measured. It is supplied by the protein and carbohydrate (which yield about 4 calories per gram each) and by the fat (which supplies about 9 calories per gram) present in food.

The amount of calories needed by an individual is required (*a*) for *basal metabolism*, that is, to keep the body's processes "ticking over", (*b*) for the miscellaneous activities of daily life and (*c*) for the day's work.

If the day's diet provides insufficient calories for a person's needs, that person will be *hungry* and will become thin; if the day's diet provides too many calories for a man's daily output of physical activity, he will become fat.

CHAPTER SIX

MINERALS

A LONG list of mineral substances plays a part in the structure of the body or in its functioning and must therefore be provided by the food and drink of a properly balanced diet. The minerals can be divided into three groups, according to the general type of physiological purpose they serve:

1. **As constituents of the body tissues.** Minerals in this group include phosphorus, iron, sulphur, zinc and copper present in muscle, blood corpuscles, liver or special structures.

2. **As soluble salts needed to maintain the constancy of the body fluids.** Important in this group are sodium, potassium and chlorine.

3. **As constituents of the skeletal structure.** Some of the minerals in bones and teeth are calcium, phosphorus, magnesium and fluorine.

In addition to the various inorganic elements mentioned above, there are a number of others which must be provided by a good diet and which each plays a specific part in the chemical mechanism of the body. *Iodine* is a constituent of the active substances in the thyroid gland in the neck which controls the rate at which energy is used up in the body processes. If the thyroid gland is deranged because of too much or too little iodine or for other reasons so that it becomes overactive, extreme restlessness accompanied by prominent eyes, and loss of weight may occur, while an inactive thyroid may cause a slowing down of both mind and body. *Copper* is needed in small but sufficient amount together with iron, for the formation of blood cells. *Manganese* plays a part in the controlled release of energy in the cells during the combustion of fuel compounds derived from food. *Cobalt* is another necessary trace mineral; it is active as part of the complex of compounds by means of which an adequate supply of new blood corpuscles is manufactured within the body.

MINERAL ELEMENTS IN THE BODY TISSUES

Life is a chemical function, but it is a process of considerable complexity. The release of energy from the nutrients supplied by food is achieved in a number of stages. Similarly, the building up of body tissue from amino acids, some of which are derived complete from food and some of which are synthesised within the cells of the body, also takes place in a number of steps. Each of these steps is rendered possible by an appropriately designed "shoe horn". These substances, that facilitate all the numerous intermediate chemical changes that together make up the life process are called *enzymes*. We shall return to them again in Chapter 10 but meanwhile it is useful to remember that particular mineral elements are essential to a number of the enzymes in the body tissues.

Sulphur. Sulphur is a component of several essential enzymes. It occurs in certain amino acids and is consequently obtained in the diet from *protein foods*. Animal proteins are richer in sulphur than seed proteins, for example, the gluten in bread. Sulphur is part of two of the *B-vitamins*, thiamine and biotin. *Insulin*, the substance that regulates the amount of sugar present in the bloodstream, is rich in sulphur. Sulphur is also present in peculiarly high concentration in *hair*. As far as is known, the customary diets eaten in the Western world adequately supply the body's needs for sulphur. Nevertheless, the possibility cannot entirely be ignored that in some circumstances additional sulphur in an appropriate form, for example, as supplied by *onions*, may contribute to nutritional well-being.

Zinc. Zinc is also a component of one of the enzymes by which life is mediated. Small amounts of zinc are present in the blood and traces are found in normal human tissues. Most ordinary diets almost certainly provide enough zinc for the body's requirements.

Iodine. Iodine is a component of one tissue of the body only and that is the thyroid gland. The importance of a knowledge of this function of iodine in the maintenance of a healthy physiological state lies in the fact that a *dietary shortage of iodine may occur* and is a possibility to be remembered. The following sources contribute iodine to the diet:

1. Water used for drinking and cooking makes a major contribution of iodine provided it is derived from an appropriate geological formation.

2. Sea fish and shell fish.

3. Certain vegetables, and especially watercress and onions, but again it is necessary for these to have been grown on soils naturally containing iodine.

There are some parts of England, notably Cumberland, Yorkshire, Derbyshire, Gloucestershire and Somerset, certain places in America, parts of Switzerland and a number of other countries, usually situated far from the sea, where the soil and consequently the drinking water and the local vegetables are deficient in iodine. In these places, *goitre* due to lack of iodine will occur among the population unless steps are taken to prevent it. The most effective preventive action is the use of sea salt or *iodised salt*, containing 1 part of iodine artificially added to each 100,000 parts of salt, for cooking and on the table.

Cobalt. The surprising discovery was made in 1948 that cobalt was a component of the substance, *vitamin B*$_{12}$, also called *cyanocobalamin*. This is an essential vitamin for the maintenance of a healthy blood supply and also has a function in growth. Cobalt, although it is a constituent of *vitamin B*$_{12}$ is required in exceedingly small amounts and it is highly unlikely that any normal diet would be deficient. Cobalt occurs in traces in a wide variety of foods, in cooking utensils and is also present in minute amounts in the atmosphere of industrial cities.

SOLUBLE MINERAL SALTS THAT MAINTAIN THE CONSTANCY OF THE BODY FLUIDS

It is a generally accepted theory that man has evolved from some remote primitive creature that lived millions of years ago in the sea. The cellular fluid of this early ancestor was similar to the composition of sea water as it then was and consequently contained the following elements and some others as did the sea which supported its life:

Chlorine	Sulphur
Sodium	Nitrogen
Magnesium	Potassium
Calcium	Iodine

Salt (sodium chloride). Salt is a nutrient that has an immediate and direct effect on nutrition. The liquid part of the bloodstream and the principal other body fluids contain about 0·9% of salt. It is essential for life that this amount be maintained within quite narrow limits. If the concentration of salt falls by any material proportion *muscular cramps* almost immediately occur.

The daily amount of salt needed by an adult is about 4

grams but this may vary quite widely for a number of reasons. Salt is eaten as such at the table or obtained from foods like bread and cheese to which it is added during manufacture. Salt is lost from the body in two principal ways:

(i) when the amount of salt consumed is sufficiently large to cause an increase in the precise concentration of 0·9% required in the blood, the excess is excreted in the urine through the kidneys.

(ii) salt is also lost to the body in sweat.

The salt lost through the kidneys is only that not required by the body; on the other hand, loss of salt in sweat may reduce the total amount sufficiently to cause a physiological shortage. Extra salt is, therefore, required in the diet (a) when hard work causing sweating is done, particularly in hot surroundings. (b) in hot climates.

Potassium. Potassium is similar in its chemical behaviour to sodium and it behaves similarly in the body. The principal difference is, however, that whereas common salt, that is sodium chloride, remains free in the body fluids, potassium chloride is retained within the cells of the tissues and the blood corpuscles. Potassium, like sodium is controlled by the action of the kidneys and any surplus is excreted in the urine. Very little potassium, however, is lost in sweat.

People eating the normal types of mixed Western diets are not likely to become deficient in potassium. In certain Asiatic and African countries, however, where unbalanced diets largely composed of such incomplete foods as tapioca or sago are eaten, potassium deficiency may arise. The chief features of potassium deficiency are muscular weakness and mental apathy. African children suffering from the disease, *kwashiorkor*, which is primarily due to lack of protein, have also been found to be deficient in potassium.

The approximate content of sodium and potassium in a number of common foods is shown in Table 8.

TABLE 8

Sodium and Potassium in Foods

(grams per oz.)

Sodium (as salt)			Potassium	
Salty foods			**Higher content**	
Corned beef		0·6	Dried fruit	0·2
Kippers		0·3	Chocolate	0·1
Cheese		0·2	Meat	0·1
Bread		0·2	Fish	0·05
Butter		0·2	Vegetables	0·05
Moderate salt content			**Moderate content**	
Eggs		0·06	Bread	0·04
Meat		0·03	Rice	0·04
Fish		0·03	Milk	0·04
Vegetables		0·03	Eggs	0·04
Oatmeal		0·01	Fruit	0·03
Low in salt			**Low content**	
Fruit		0·004	Beer	0·01
Rice		0·004	Margarine	0·01
Flour	less than	0·002	Tapioca	0·006
Sago	less than	0·002	Butter	0·005
Sugar		trace	Sugar	trace

Although other mineral substances, notably calcium and magnesium, must be present in exactly appropriate concentration to maintain the uniformity of the composition of the body fluid, they can more conveniently be considered as constituents of the skeleton.

MINERAL COMPONENTS OF THE SKELETAL STRUCTURE

The most important mineral substance in teeth and bones, from the point of view of the nutritionist, are calcium and phosphorus. These substances are discussed in more detail in Chapter 7.

Magnesium

Magnesium is of great importance in the functioning of the body and in biological experiments where magnesium is artificially withdrawn life is quickly brought to a stop. As was mentioned above, a small, steady concentration of magnesium is always present in the bloodstream. Most of the body's store of magnesium, however, is present in the bones in combination with phosphorus.

From the point of view of the nutritionist, magnesium is a substance of no concern. The total amount needed in an adult's body is only about 1 oz. and it is present in almost every kind of food. Green vegetables all contain magnesium in significant amounts because it is an essential component of the green pigment, chlorophyll.

Fluorine. Traces of fluorine are present in bones and teeth and in other tissues of the body, notably in the skin and the thyroid gland. The consumption of from 2 to 3 mg.* in the daily intake of food and drink is required for the maintenance of good teeth free from dental caries. *A moderate excess* of fluorine in the diet causes mottling of the teeth. *A large excess* of fluorine is poisonous. Fluorine is obtained in the diet from the following sources:

1. **Drinking water.** A good water supply contains 1 part of fluorine per million; soft waters may contain no fluorine while very hard waters may contain up to 10 p.p.m.

* mg. is the abbreviation for milligram; 1000 mg. = 1 g. (gram); 28.4 g. = 1 oz.

Maldon in Essex is remarkable for the high proportion of fluorine in the drinking water. Mottling of the teeth is very noticeable in the Maldon population.

2. **Sea Fish** may contain 5 to 10 p.p.m. of fluorine.

3. **Tea (particularly china tea)** may contain up to 100 p.p.m. in its dry form.

The most straightforward method of providing an adequate dietary supply of fluorine in places where the water supplies are very soft is for the public health authorities to arrange for the fluorine content of the water to be adjusted to 1 p.p.m.

Other Minerals

There are a number of other mineral elements that are known to exercise a biological function, often in trace quantities, in living cells of various kinds. *Boron* is necessary for the healthy growth of certain plants; but it is not known to play a part in human well-being. *Vanadium* is a metal that is essential to the biological functioning of the sea-squirt (Ascidium). The need of this creature only for this unexpected substance seems to be a special peculiarity. Vanadium is not known to have any function in human nutrition. *Selenium* is absorbed by plants and in places where the concentration of selenium in the soil is high, the plants may actually become poisonous to livestock. There is some doubt whether or not traces of selenium play some part in human functions. *Cadmium*, like vanadium, has the peculiarity of being known only to contribute to the biochemistry of a single species, the scallop. It is not known to be of any importance to man.

RECAPITULATION

Although an understanding of the functions of the substances that have been referred to up till now is important to the student of nutrition, it is broadly true that besides salt (sodium chloride) and iodine and fluorine, which must be present in small but adequate amounts, the sole minerals with which a nutritionist dealing with practical problems of Western dietetics need usually be concerned in making a first assessment of the nutritional adequacy of a particular diet are:

1. Calcium
2. Phosphorus
3. Iron

These substances are therefore dealt with separately in the following chapters.

CHAPTER SEVEN

THE IMPORTANCE OF CALCIUM
AND PHOSPHORUS IN NUTRITION

THE main tissues of the body, the flesh and blood of which we are constructed, are composed of a chemical network of carbon atoms, diversified here and there with nitrogen and sulphur. This is the basic organic structure. Our flesh, with its resilient elastic quality, is composed of what in technical terms are called *polymers*, and which we in ordinary language usually describe as *plastics*. It is not an accident that flesh is *rubbery*. Its chemical configuration shares with rubber (and with artificial plastics made by man) a polymerised structure. It is true, of course, that living tissues with their ability for self-regeneration and movement, their capacity to utilise components derived from food and their mechanisms for combusting nutrients for energy, are far more complex than any artificial plastic so far made. The small amounts of many of the mineral substances described in the last chapter are essential for certain of the synthetic processes and for the energy-release mechanisms in the living body. But apart from the tissues of the muscles and organs of the body, there is the quite different structure of the teeth and skeleton.

The hard substance of the bones and teeth is largely composed of *calcium phosphate*, which is as its name implies a compound of calcium and phosphorus. The body of an adult man or woman normally contains from 2 *to* $3\frac{1}{2}$ *lb. of calcium* of which at least 99% is present in the skeleton. This substantial quantity of calcium, all of which comes from the diet, is not fixed and static in its position in bones and teeth. During the processes of growth there is a constant coming and going of calcium being laid down into the structure of bones and at the same time being withdrawn into the bloodstream and fluids for use elsewhere in the body.

CALCIUM

In considering the needs of the body for calcium from the diet and the different foods from which these requirements are to be supplied it is not sufficient merely to know how much calcium is present. The following considerations must all be kept in mind:

1. the total amount of calcium present in all the different components of the diet

2. the presence of factors assisting the absorption of calcium, these are:
    i. *vitamin D*
    ii. *proteins*

3. the presence of factors interfering with the absorption of calcium, these are:
    i. *phytic acid*
    ii. *fats*
    iii. *oxalic acid*

Sources of Calcium in the Diet

Table 9 shows the relative calcium content of a selection of common foods. It can be seen from this table that the foods that contribute substantial amounts of calcium to the diet are (*a*) milk and cheese, (*b*) fish, particularly such fish as sardine, whitebait and sometimes tinned salmon where one eats the bones, and (*c*) some green vegetables (but not spinach). "Hard" drinking water may provide significant amounts of dietary calcium.

TABLE 9

The Calcium Content of Foods
(mg. per oz.)

Cheese—hard, e.g. Cheddar	250	Watercress	65
Cheese—soft, e.g.		Cabbage	20
Camenbert	100	Turnip	15
Condensed milk	80	Potato	2
Milk—fresh	35		
Whitebait	240	Meat	5
Sardine	110		
Salmon—canned	85	Flour—white	5
Herring	30	Bread—white	4
White fish	8	Rice	2

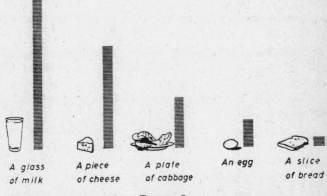

FIGURE 8.

The calcium in normal servings of different foods.

Factors Assisting the Absorption of Calcium

The presence of *vitamin D* in the diet or its formation in the skin by the action of sunshine assists the body to absorb calcium from foodstuffs through the digestive tract and into the bloodstream. Vitamin D is discussed in more detail in Chapter 12.

The readiness with which calcium is absorbed into the body is facilitated by the presence of *protein* in the digestive tract at the same time. This underlines the importance of a mixed diet in nutrition. We shall be discussing in Chapter 14 the varying amounts of each of the different nutrients required for adequate nutrition. It is quite possible to assess in quantitative terms how much protein and calcium and phosphorus and iron, and all the other nutrients are required. Nevertheless, a good diet must be composed of foods, and in many respects the total effect of a properly "balanced" mixture of foods may be greater than the arithmetical sum of its individual components. The beneficial effect of the presence of protein in the gut on the simultaneous absorption of calcium is an example of this principle.

Calcium in the Blood

Although the bloodstream is in one respect merely the transport route along which calcium passes from the intestines into the bones, nevertheless a small but uniform amount of calcium must always be present in the blood. If the amount of calcium in the bloodstream becomes too low the following effects occur:

(a) *Tetany*. The nerves become too easily stimulated and cramps, particularly of the hands and feet, occur.
(b) *Loss of muscle tone*. A normal level of blood calcium is necessary for the functioning of the muscles.
(c) *Blood clotting*. The presence of calcium is necessary for the normal process of blood clotting to occur.

Note. In adults, an inadequate supply of calcium in the diet is not likely to cause a reduction in the level of calcium in the blood because in healthy people the bones form a reservoir of calcium from which the body can draw to maintain a uniform concentration in the circulation. The *parathyroid gland*, which is a small organ in the neck attached to the thyroid, acts as the regulator by which the exact level of calcium required is always maintained in the blood. Only if the parathyroid becomes diseased or damaged does the amount of calcium in the blood fall and tetany, which may prove fatal, occur.

Substances Interfering with the Absorption of Calcium

Phytic acid is an organic phosphorus compound. It possesses the property of interfering with the absorption of calcium. This is shown by the fact that calcium is absorbed less efficiently from a diet containing a large amount of brown bread than from the same diet with white bread substituted for brown. This is because brown bread contains more phytic acid. It has also been shown that the disease, *rickets*, which arises from unsatisfactory deposition of calcium in the bones of young children (and young animals), occurs more readily when foods such as brown bread, oatmeal or beans, which contain comparatively large amounts of phytic acid, constitute a major part of the diet.

The following foods contribute phytic acid to the diet:

	Phytic acid (mg. P per oz.)
Oatmeal	75
Dried peas and beans	65
Nuts (almonds, brazils, cobnuts)	50
Wholemeal bread	25
White bread	3

The addition of calcium to bread to counteract the effect of phytic acid. In order to counteract the effect of phytic acid in hampering the absorption of calcium, the British Government, on the recommendation of the Medical Research Council, made a regulation to enforce the addition of 14 oz. of *creta preparata* (a specially purified form of chalk, i.e. calcium carbonate) to each 280 lb. sack of flour used for breadmaking.

There are two important factors to be borne in mind in considering the practical significance of phytic acid in nutrition:

(*a*) Not all the phytic acid originally present in uncooked food survives the processes of cooking.

(*b*) Although the introduction of foods containing phytic acid into the diet undoubtedly reduces the amount of available calcium, people who have subsisted for a long time on diets containing these foods appear to be able to adapt themselves quite satisfactorily to them and to obtain sufficient calcium for their nutritional needs.

These two considerations show once again that although it is possible to draw up a table of nutritional requirements for different types of people listing the various quantities of protein and calories and vitamins and calcium (as will be discussed in detail in Chapter 14), nevertheless the body possesses a number of self-correcting mechanisms—such as this ability to adapt itself to reduced calcium and increased phytic acid—and foods can contain mixtures of nutrients which together possess properties somewhat different from those made up of the sum of their individual components.

Fats, and particularly "saturated" fats such as lard, mutton fat and suet, may interfere to some degree with the absorption of calcium. This is unlikely to be of any practical significance for well people but may be of importance to patients suffering from diseases in which the normal efficiency of digestion is affected.

Oxalic acid occurs in small proportions in some leafy vegetables, notably *spinach* and *rhubarb*. Like phytic acid, it combines with calcium and this interferes with its absorption.

Thus, although by chemical analysis spinach can be shown to contain a moderately large amount of calcium none of this appears to be available to the body.

Another way in which the absorption of calcium from the diet may be prevented is by the constant consumption of *Epsom salts* (magnesium sulphate). The calcium is converted into calcium sulphate which is insoluble.

The Practical Effects of Insufficient Calcium in the Diet

1. *On unborn babies*. The unborn child is never short of calcium because it is able to draw upon the calcium in its mother's bones if her diet is deficient.

2. *Expectant mothers*. Shortage of dietary calcium can be almost immediately harmful. "For every child a tooth" is a saying implying that mothers whose diet during pregnancy is inadequate in calcium lose their teeth. In extreme shortage the disease, *osteomalacia* (softening of the bones), may occur.

3. *Nursing mothers*. Since mother's milk contains substantial amounts of calcium, a woman has need of adequate calcium in her diet when she is nursing a baby. Dietary shortage at this time may also be associated with loss of teeth.

4. *Children and adolescents*. Restriction of calcium may hamper growth. In young children inadequate absorption of calcium may lead to *rickets*.

5. *Adults*. It is possible that long-continued shortage of calcium may have some bearing on the health of the teeth in adults. Old people often suffer from a withdrawal of calcium from their bones with consequent brittleness of the bones. "Rheumatic" pains may also be due to the effect of chronic shortage of calcium in the joints. It is very doubtful, however, whether these symptoms are directly attributable to nutrition. More probably they arise from a failure of the body's hormone system to maintain the appropriate internal environment.

PHOSPHORUS

Phosphorus, usually in the chemical form of phosphates, is an essential mineral for the functioning of the life processes of the body. It is also a component of many of the substances of which the body is composed.

(a) Phosphorus plays an essential part in the processes by which the body obtains energy from food.

(b) It is essential in maintaining the constancy of the body fluids.

(c) It is a major component, with calcium, of bones and teeth.

Phosphorus occurs in most common foods and it is highly unlikely, therefore, that any ordinary diet will ever provide too little. (Under exceptional circumstances, a harmful deficiency of phosphorus can occur in *cattle* grazing on inadequate pastures.)

The Phosphorus Content of Different Foods

Glandular meats, for example, sweetbread, kidney and liver, and brains are very rich in phosphorus. Dairy produce, particularly cheese, also contains substantial amounts. Since, as I have stated above, phosphorus is essential to biological life, it is present in almost all foods, since they themselves were at one time alive. Where articles of diet are highly purified during the course of preparation—sugar is, of course, an outstanding example—the amount of phosphorus becomes reduced.

In considering the total amount of phosphorus which any particular food contains, however, it must once again be remembered that not all the phosphorus may be available to the body. For example, "wholemeal" flour (which usually comprises about 85% of the total grain) may contain 70 mg.

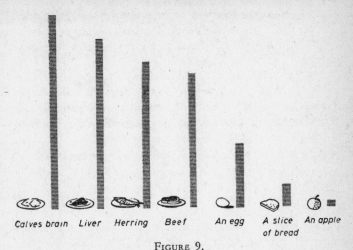

FIGURE 9.

The amount of phosphorus in normal servings of different foods.

of phosphorus per oz., but of this about half is phytic acid phosphorus which may not be absorbed.

Although all this is of interest, it must again be pointed out that in terms of practical nutrition, there is no need for concern since a shortage of phosphorus is hardly possible under any circumstance likely to be encountered.

Phosphates for "Strength" and for "the Brain"

Not long after it had been discovered, early in the present century, that phosphorus plays a part in the production of energy in muscle it was suggested that the provision of *additional* phosphorus would therefore *increase* the amount of muscular work a man could do. On the strength of this notion the German authorities in World War I provided a phosphate drink for large numbers of soldiers and workmen.

Unfortunately, the idea was wrong and it is now agreed that supplementary phosphate, whether taken as food, as a drink, or in tablets does not contribute in any way to a man's capacity to work or to his resistance to fatigue.

Another fallacy arose from the discovery that brain tissue contains a high proportion of phosphorus. This led to the suggestion that foods high in phosphorus, and notably fish, would be "good for the brain". It is regrettable that this also is not so.

CHAPTER EIGHT

IRON

WHEREAS a knowledge of the function of phosphorus in the tissues of the body and its origin in the foods that constitute the diet is interesting and gives us an understanding of an essential aspect of the life chemistry upon which our activity and well-being depend, it is not of much practical concern to the nutritionist who is concerned with the provision of diets for a modern industrial community. On the other hand, the mineral, *iron*, is of very direct concern to the working nutritionist. Iron is of great importance in human nutrition and iron deficiency is a common cause of ill-health in many parts of the world.

The body of a healthy adult contains from 4 to 5 grams of iron; this is about $\frac{1}{7}$ oz. of the metal. The iron in the body is distributed in three principal types of compound.

1. **Haemoglobin.** Haemoglobin is the pigment that gives blood its redness. This pigment is of quite peculiar importance since it possesses the chemical property of being able to combine with oxygen as the blood passes through the complex series of vessels that constitute the spongy, open structure of the lungs. The heart then pumps this oxygenated blood throughout the body. It is this oxygen, conveyed attached to the iron-containing pigment, haemoglobin, that makes possible the "combustion" of fuel provided by food upon which we depend for energy. During this "combustion" in our muscles the oxygen is utilised to form carbon dioxide gas (CO_2). Haemoglobin is capable of combining with CO_2 just as it previously did with oxygen. In this way the blood,

returning again to the lungs, is able to carry the CO_2 with it and discharge it in the expired breath. If the diet contains insufficient iron, the amount of circulating haemoglobin is reduced and *anaemia* results. About 60 to 70% of the total iron in the body is combined as haemoglobin.

Haemoglobin is not loose in the blood but is carried in the *red blood corpuscles*. The life of each corpuscle is about six weeks. At the end of that time the corpuscles break down and the iron is released. Only a small amount of it escapes from the body however. Most of it is used again for the formation of fresh corpuscles. The new blood cells are produced in the marrow of the bones.

Iron is lost from the body in two main ways:

(*a*) by the general wear and tear of the body cells and in the remains of digestive juices passed out in faeces, and

(*b*) by bleeding due either to injury, from bleeding haemorrhoids, or in the monthly blood loss occurring in women.

If the diet does not provide enough iron to make good these losses anaemia will occur.

2. **Tissue iron.** A proportion of the total iron in the body occurs in the tissues combined in protein where it forms part of the enzyme system by means of which the combustion of fuel derived from foodstuffs takes place in the presence of oxygen brought in from the lungs. These protein-iron compounds are not affected by diet but remain constant regardless of any dietary privations to which the body may be submitted.

3. **Storage iron.** About one-seventh of the total amount of iron present in a normal healthy adult occurs as a complex protein compound called *ferritin*. This provides an emergency store upon which the body can call during short periods of deficiency.

FOODS CONTRIBUTING IRON IN THE DIET

Since iron is primarily required in the human body as a constituent of the red blood cells and since it is stored in a complex combination with muscle protein and also in liver, the foods richest in iron are blood (when eaten as "black pudding"), liver and meat (which is, of course, the muscular tissue of cattle, sheep or pigs—or, for that matter, horse or goat where these animals are used as food). Characteristic figures are shown below in Table 10.

As can be seen from the table, meats of all sorts are richest in iron and of all meats kidney and, particularly, liver contain high concentrations of iron. This is because iron is stored in the liver of animals, as it is in our own livers. Since the principal function of iron in the body is as part of the molecule of haemoglobin, the essential component of red blood, it is obvious therefore that foods made out of blood, that is blood sausage and black pudding, should contain substantial amounts of iron.

Useful amounts of nutritionally valuable iron may be obtained from iron cooking-pots and other kitchen utensils and from rusty water. The quite exceptionally high concentration of iron in curry powder is derived in this way from the equipment in which the powder is prepared.

In considering the significance of different foods in the diet as sources of iron, it is particularly important, not only to be aware of the amount of iron present in 1 oz. of each foodstuff, shown in the table, but also to bear in mind the normal quantity of each article likely to be consumed each day. Although curry powder contains 21 mg. of iron per ounce and black pudding 5·6 mg., most ordinary diets are more likely to contain regular amounts of meat and eggs and wholemeal bread than they are to include curry or blood sausage.

While meat, eggs and whole grain cereals are good sources

TABLE 10

THE IRON CONTENT OF CERTAIN COMMON FOODS
(mg. per oz.)

Meat		Vegetables	
"Black pudding" (blood sausage)	5·6	Spinach	0·9
Liver	3·8	Peas, green	0·5
Kidney	3·8	Watercress	0·4
Beef, corned	3·0	Cabbage	0·3
Beef	1·1	Carrot	0·2
Mutton	0·6	Potato	0·2
Pork	0·3	Onion ⎫	
		Tomato ⎬	0·1
		Turnip ⎭	

Fish		Pulses	
Sardine	1·0	Lentils	2·2
Kipper	0·6	Haricot beans	1·9
Herring	0·4	Dried peas	1·3
Salmon	0·4		
Cod, white fish	0·3	Fruit	
		Dried apricots	1·2
		Dried figs	1·2

Dairy produce		Prunes	0·8
Eggs	0·8	Raisins	0·5
Cheese	0·2	Blackcurrants	0·4
Milk ⎫		Apples ⎫	
Butter ⎬ less than	0·1	Pears	
		Plums ⎬	0·1
		Oranges	
Cereals		Lemons	
Oatmeal	1·4	Melon ⎭	
Flour, wholemeal	1·0		
Flour, white	0·4	Miscellaneous	
Bread, wholemeal	0·7	Curry powder	21·0
Bread, white	0·2	Cocoa	4·1
Barley	0·2	Chocolate	0·9
Rice	0·2	Peanuts	0·7

of iron, it is important to note that milk, though rich in protein, calcium and numerous vitamins is almost completely lacking in iron. It is, therefore, particularly important to ensure that babies and invalids who for other reasons may find a diet made up to a large degree of milk desirable shall be provided in due time with an appropriate source of iron.

THE ABSORPTION OF IRON INTO THE BODY

Although it is important that the diet should contain an adequate amount of iron, it is a remarkable fact that only a small proportion of the total iron present in the foods eaten is absorbed; the greater part is eliminated in the faeces. Furthermore, the availability of iron to the body differs depending on the chemical combination in which it is present in different foods. For example, whereas about one-tenth of the iron present in a mixed diet is absorbed, about twice as much, that is one-fifth, is taken into the body from beef.

The following factors affect the proportion of the iron consumed that is actually absorbed:

1. **Whether or not the body is already deficient in iron.** Medicinal iron, that is the iron in iron-containing formulae, tablets of iron phosphate and the like, is absorbed in greatly increased proportion by people who are suffering from anaemia when compared with the amounts of iron absorbed by people whose body already contains an adequate store of iron. The way in which the gut of healthy people is able to prevent the absorption of dietary iron, whereas the gut of anaemic patients allows iron to pass through into the bloodstream is not properly understood. And the situation is even more puzzling from the fact that iron from eggs or liver is absorbed no better by anaemic people than by those whose nutritional state is fully satisfactory.

2. **The chemical combination in which iron occurs in different foods.** Although the principal function of iron in

the body is the formation of haemoglobin, the red pigment in blood, iron already combined in this way in foods is particularly poorly absorbed. Thus, while blood sausage is at the top of the list in Table 10 so far as the total amount of iron in it is concerned, this iron is only utilised by the body to a very small extent.

3. **The presence of phytic acid.** Phytic acid forms insoluble compounds with iron just as it does with calcium. It follows, therefore, that some of the iron present in wholemeal bread and other foods containing phytic acid will be prevented from being absorbed. The addition of more calcium will neutralise the phytic acid and prevent it from interfering in this way.

4. **The presence of vitamin C (ascorbic acid).** The presence of foods containing vitamin C, e.g. green vegetables and fruit, in the same meals as those providing sources of iron assists the body to absorb the iron better.

5. **The presence of protein.** It is important to note that iron is absorbed more readily if the foods from which the diet is composed also contribute protein. *This underlines the cardinal principle of good nutrition: it is that an adequate diet made up of a proper mixture of components is often better than the sum of the individual nutrients of which it is composed.*

Apart from the direct effect which proteins exert in assisting the absorption of iron, it also appears that the iron present in the form of *ferritin* is better absorbed than iron in other chemical conbinations. Ferritin, it will be remembered, is a compound in which iron is stored in the tissues and it therefore constitutes a significant proportion of the iron present in such foods as meat and liver.

A sixth factor that is known to affect the facility with which the body takes up iron from the diet is a deficiency of a vitamin of the B-group called *pyridoxin* (vitamin B_6). We shall discuss this vitamin in more detail in Chapter 10. It is not very likely that pyridoxin deficiency has any bearing on nutritional health under normal circumstances. The fact remains, however, that a shortage of pyridoxin in the diet causes the absorption of iron to become *too rapid* so that excessive amounts of iron accumulate in the body.

TOO MUCH IRON

Siderosis is the name given to the rather uncommon condition that arises when *too much iron* is absorbed into the body. Siderosis may arise in two ways:

(*a*) as a rare hereditary disease usually occurring in men over forty-five. The symptoms are cirrhosis of the liver, diabetes and sometimes skin discoloration as well.

(*b*) an inadequate diet, lacking in *phosphorus* which, as phytic acid, interferes with iron absorption, but containing grossly too much iron may cause siderosis. The most striking examples occur among the Bantus of South Africa who consume more than ten times as much iron as they need from the iron cooking-pots they use. The people at the same time eat a poor diet largely made up of maize and deficient in phosphorus.

Although under most normal circumstances excess iron taken into the body passes through without being absorbed, there are very occasionally reports of medicinal supplements of iron, taken for example as ferrous sulphate tablets, causing toxic symptoms of poisoning. This is, however, almost always restricted to children.

RECAPITULATION

1. Practical nutritionists need to take notice that the diets in which they are interested contain sufficient iron. This attention is required because what appear to be ordinary mixtures of food may supply insufficient iron.

2. A deficiency of iron in the diet can lead to anaemia. Anaemia is one of the commonest deficiency diseases in all parts of the world. Although there are a number of different kinds of anaemia, by far the commonest is that due to an inadequate amount of iron in the diet. The most obvious features of anaemia are (*a*) fatigue and lassitude (*b*) breathlessness (*c*) headache (*d*) insomnia (*e*) dyspepsia (*f*) "pins and needles" in the feet and hands.

3. Foods rich in iron which is capable of being absorbed and thus able to prevent the appearance of iron-deficiency anaemia are:

> Meat (and particularly liver)
> Eggs
> Oatmeal
> Peas and beans
> Wholemeal bread

4. Loss of iron from the body, which in consequence raises the requirement for iron from the diet, arises from the following causes:

(*a*) loss of blood from accident or haemorrhoids in men or from menstruation in women.

(*b*) extra iron required by expectant mothers to supply the unborn child; losses during the birth of an infant; and iron losses in milk by nursing mothers.

(*c*) general wear and tear of the body and loss in the remains of digestive juices passed out in faeces.

5. Nutritionally valuable amounts of iron which can contribute significantly to the main supplies derived from diet:

(*a*) are contained in iron-containing drinking water

(*b*) are derived from iron cooking vessels and utensils.

CHAPTER NINE

VITAMIN A

THE main bulk of nutrients of which an adequate diet is composed are *carbohydrates, proteins* and *fats*. Besides these, a number of *inorganic mineral substances* are required, including salt, calcium and phosphorus compounds and the various others that have been discussed in Chapters 6, 7 and 8. But in addition to these there is a group of organic compounds, each with a particular type of chemical configuration, which are needed by the body if the diet is to maintain adequate nutrition: these substances are *the vitamins*.

Vitamin A is soluble in fats and, in consequence, is not soluble in water. It is found in the fats of foods of animal origin, e.g. in cod-liver oil, in the fatty component of liver and kidney, in butter and in cheese containing fat, in eggs and in other food to which reference is made below.

The yellow pigment *carotene*, present in carrots and in a number of other vegetable foods including green vegetables, apricots and tomatoes is similar in chemical configuration to vitamin A and possesses *vitamin A activity* when eaten.

THE FUNCTIONS OF VITAMIN A
IN THE BODY

1. Vitamin A is needed for the proper functioning of the cells of the body but the way in which it works and the purpose it serves are not fully understood.

2. It is necessary for the proper growth and health of

children; it is concerned in the growth of bone and the formation of teeth.

3. It is required for the health of the skin, the cornea of the eye (that is the outer surface of the eyeball) and for the linings of the respiratory tract, the throat and the bronchial tubes.

4. The only tissue for which the precise nature of the function of vitamin A is known is the retina of the eye (that is the sensitive "photographic film" where light is actually perceived at the back of the eye). The ability to see in a dim light is due to the presence of a chemical pigment in the eye called *rhodopsin*. The purple colour of this pigment is bleached when light falls on it. When vitamin A is available, the pigment is regenerated so that it is available to record the next picture. It follows, therefore, that when the diet is deficient and vitamin A is lacking, the ability to see in a dim light is reduced. This condition is called *night-blindness*.

SOURCES OF VITAMIN A-ACTIVITY IN THE DIET

The vitamin A-activity of the foods listed below in Table 11 are given in terms of *international units*. This is a convenient way of expressing the biological activity of the vitamin A present as such in animal food and of the activity of carotene provided by vegetable food. The conversion of carotene to vitamin A in the body is not complete so that the expression of the vitamin A-activity content of foods is most satisfactorily measured in international units as shown. As a general rule, the carotene content of green vegetables and their consequent vitamin A-activity runs broadly parallel to their greenness. From this it follows that dark green vegetables such as spinach and watercress have a higher vitamin activity than the white hearts of cabbage or lettuce.

TABLE 11

THE AVERAGE VITAMIN A-ACTIVITY OF CERTAIN FOODS
(International units per oz.)

Fish oils and fatty fish		Fruit and vegetables	
Halibut-liver oil	600,000	Carrots	4,000
Shark-liver oil	35,000	Spinach	1,500
Cod-liver oil	30,000	Watercress	500
Sardine	80	Apricots (dried)	470
Salmon	70	Tomato	300
Herring	40	Prunes (dried)	240
		Cabbage	85
Meats		Bananas	60
Ox liver	6,000	Green peas	50
Sheep liver	6,000	Orange juice	50
Kidney	280	Potato, onion	nil
Beef	15		
Mutton	15		
Dairy produce			
Butter	1,200		
Margarine (vitaminised)	600		
Cheese	350		
Eggs	280		
Milk	30		

Note. An international unit is the activity of 0·3 micrograms, i.e. 0·3 ten thousandths of a gram, of the pure chemical vitamin A* as it occurs in animal foods. This same activity is produced by twice the weight, that is 0.6 micrograms, of beta-carotene. Beta-carotene is one of the several similar pigments which occur in carrots and also in green vegetables.

It can be seen from the items that do *not* appear in the table above that many common foods, including bread, flour,

* Now more accurately expressed in terms of "retinol equivalents".

sugar, suet and cooking fat, contribute *no vitamin A* to the diet, neither do potatoes nor onions, and meat only contains a small amount. It consequently follows that a varied diet in which not only butter, vitaminised margarine, eggs and cheese but also green vegetables and occasional servings of carrots or liver are included, should be eaten in order to maintain an adequate consumption of vitamin A.

HARMFUL EFFECTS OF TOO LITTLE VITAMIN A

Considerable amounts of vitamin A can be stored away in one's liver. This is the reason why the livers of animals used for meat are rich in vitamin A. Because of these stores a previously well-fed person may live without harm for several months on a diet deficient in the vitamin or even one in which it is entirely absent. Eventually, however, a shortage of vitamin A becomes apparent in two ways:

1. "*Night blindness*" will occur, that is a failure in the ability of one's eyes to become adapted to a dim light. (It is important to note, however, that "night-blindness" can occur for a number of reasons other than a shortage of vitamin A. Hence, although prolonged shortage of vitamin A will cause "night blindness", this condition, of itself, may not be due to vitamin A-deficiency.)

2. A peculiar roughness of the skin, particularly of the outer surfaces of the upper arm and on the fronts of the thighs, called "*follicular keratosis*" may occur. (Again it must be said, that although long-continued shortage of vitamin A in the diet *sometimes* causes follicular keratosis, some people suffer from this condition for other reasons quite unrelated to nutrition.)

3. If children are eating a diet deficient in vitamin A, they will not "do well" and their growth will be checked.

VITAMIN A WILL NOT PREVENT INFECTION

If animals, particularly experimental rats, are fed on a ration which does not contain vitamin A, their skin undergoes certain harmful changes and their tear glands become blocked so that the front surface of their eyes (the cornea) dries up. This condition is called *xerophthalmia*. The unnatural dryness of the eyes makes them susceptible to infection and, indeed, if the vitamin A-deficiency is prolonged, the invading infection may damage the rat's eyes beyond repair. Vitamin A shortage in rats also causes changes in the lining of their bronchial tubes which may eventually lead to death from broncho-pneumonia. If vitamin A is given to deficient animals before these changes have proceeded too far, the invasion by infecting micro-organisms is checked and they recover. When this was first observed, some of the early researchers used to refer to vitamin A as "the anti-infective" vitamin.

It is very important to understand:

(a) that the consumption of vitamin A by people who are already eating a good mixed diet gives them no added protection against the common infectious diseases.

(b) in spite of what the advertisements say, vitamin A has not been shown to give any special resistance to colds or influenza.

THE EFFECT OF TOO MUCH VITAMIN A

If too much vitamin A is eaten it accumulates in the body. Most of it, as has already been mentioned, is stored in the liver but some can also be stored in the muscular tissues as well. There was a case reported during World War II when carrots were recommended as a source of vitamin A-activity in place of dairy produce, fish and other foods which were scarce. A patient, who from misplaced patriotism had accustomed himself to a diet consisting principally of carrots alone, developed a peculiar yellowness of the complexion due to an overdose of carotene.

If it is consumed in grossly excessive amounts, vitamin A may be acutely toxic. The earliest evidence of the effect of too much vitamin A was obtained from the Arctic. The Eskimos had a tradition that of all the meat of the polar bear, the liver alone was poisonous. Arctic explorers who found the flesh of these bears unattractive and who ate the liver suffered from drowsiness, headache, vomiting and peeling of the skin. It was later discovered that polar bear liver contained up to 600,000 international units of vitamin A per oz., so that a meal of half a pound of it represented a dose of nearly 5 million international units.

The ill-effects suffered by explorers under the exceptional conditions of life in the Arctic have been paralleled under the more normal conditions of civilised life. Learning that vitamin A is an important component of a good diet—as indeed it is—has led a few well-meaning mothers who have been recommended to give their children an appropriate amount of some reliable source, such as cod-liver oil, to try to do even better. Hearing that there are even more concentrated sources of the vitamin, for example, halibut-liver oil which, as can be seen from Table 11 contains about twenty times as much, they have given the children as much halibut-liver oil as they had given cod-liver oil before. The effect of this has been to provide them with grossly excessive amounts of vitamin A, often for periods of months at a time. The harmful results occur as lack of appetite, irritation, a dry, itching skin, unhealthy hair and swelling over the bones of the arms and legs. *It is important to remember that although an adequate amount of each vitamin is necessary for health, more than enough contributes no advantage and, particularly with vitamins soluble in fat and insoluble in water, of which vitamin A is one, a large excess may be actively harmful.*

KERATOMALACIA

Diets containing inadequate amounts of vitamin A can be found in industrialised countries of the West. Where a reasonable variety of foodstuffs is available, however, it is uncommon to encounter a diet completely devoid of vitamin A or to see people who have lived for sufficiently prolonged periods of time on such grossly vitamin A-deficient diets that the more striking effects of deficiency can be seen. This may occur, however, and did occur in Denmark during World War I when knowledge of vitamin A was less complete and, in consequence, an unduly large proportion of dairy produce was being exported from the country. Among certain rice-eating peoples in Asia and in parts of Africa, however, diets almost devoid of vitamin A may be eaten. The results of prolonged and almost complete absence of the vitamin are the appearance of the disease, keratomalacia.

Keratomalacia is a disease in which the cornea, that is the tough, moist surface of the front of the eye, becomes softened and parts of it may become necrotic. This may lead to ulceration, perforation into the inner structures of the eye, followed by blindness. Indeed, this disease is even today a serious cause of blindness in India, China, Indonesia and certain parts of Africa. It is commonest among children.

It is important for every student to remember that there are two distinct aspects to the science of nutrition. On the one hand, in the prosperous industrial countries of the West where wide varieties of food are customarily eaten as the normal diet, the likelihood of acute shortage of a specific nutrient is quite small particularly when, as with vitamin A, substantial amounts may be stored in the body. Thus, in an environment such as that of twentieth-century Great Britain, nutritional knowledge may be more useful for avoiding popular fads or the mistaken consumption of unnecessarily large amounts of substances temporarily in the news or overstressed by advertisers. The other aspect of the subject, however, is that affecting the underfed majority of the world's population abroad where diets may be simple and consequently devoid of one or other of the several components required for adequate nutrition. In the East, keratomalacia is usually associated with poverty and famine, but it may also afflict the children of moderately well-to-do parents who through ignorance have fed them on defective dried milk preparations made from skimmed milk and almost entirely devoid of vitamin A.

If keratomalacia is treated while it is in its early stages, the sufferer recovers completely. If the damage to the eyes has advanced too far, treatment cannot save the patient from blindness or even, if serious infection has gained access, from death. *The cure is to give vitamin A, either as cod-liver oil or as halibut-liver oil or some more concentrated preparation*: It can be seen that *keratomalacia* in human beings is parallel to xerophthalmia in experimental animals, both arising from a prolonged severe deficiency of vitamin A in the diet.

FACTORS AFFECTING THE
ABSORPTION OF VITAMIN A

1. **Variation in the Vitamin A Content of Food.** All food tables must by their very nature be average approximations. For example although a figure can be given for the *average* percentage of fat, let us say, in mutton, one particular slice of mutton may vary enormously in its fattiness (that is, the proportion of fat it contains) from another. Similarly, the vitamin-A content of egg, to take an example, can vary very widely depending on the diet of the hen. Similar variations occur with other animal foods; the vitamin-A in milk is influenced by the cow's ration, and liver and butter will also vary. Similarly, the vitamin-A content of fatty fish varies

with the sexual maturity of the fish. Comment has already been made about the fluctuations around the average occurring in the vitamin A-activity of green and yellow vegetables due to changes in the amount of *carotene* in them.

2. **The State of Subdivision of Vegetables.** The carotene that gives vegetables their vitamin-A activity is contained inside the plant cells. These cells are sometimes quite resistent to cooking and to the digestive juices. It has been found that if carrots are finely homogenised in a mechanical blender, their vitamin-A activity is very markedly increased.

3. **Protection of Vitamin A by Vitamin E.** Vitamin E, which is described in Chapter 12, protects vitamin A and carotene against destruction by the oxygen of the atmosphere. The vitamin-A activity of foods that also contain vitamin E is, therefore, more stable. Similarly, vitamin A can be stored more readily in the liver if adequate amounts of vitamin E are also present in the diet.

4. **Harmful Effect of Mineral Oil.** When edible fats are treated under appropriate conditions with alkali, for example, caustic soda or caustic potash, they become split into *glycerol* and *soap*. This process is called *saponification*. Since both glycerol and fat are soluble in water, saponification facilitates the absorption of fat into the body. In fats that contain vitamin A, the comparatively minute proportion, by weight, of vitamin A remains in the *unsaponifiable fraction* when the fat is treated with alkali. *Mineral oils*, such as liquid paraffin which at one time used to be taken as a laxative, and *greases*, such as vaseline, which—most unwisely—have been included in made-up articles of diet, until banned by law, *cannot be saponified*. They are unavailable to the body for the production of energy and do not qualify to be classified as food. Worse still, they reduce the absorption of carotene and vitamin A, consumed at the same time.

CHAPTER TEN

THE VITAMIN B GROUP OF NUTRIENTS

THERE are a number of vitamins, all of which are soluble in water, which are quite often, although by no means always, found together in the same foods. It is not certain that all the individual substances which combine to produce the state of good nutrition and health known to be due to the B-group of vitamins provided by an adequate diet have been identified yet. The members of the group of most importance to practical nutritionists are the following:

1. *Vitamin B_1*, also called *aneurin* in Great Britain and *thiamine* in America.

2. *Riboflavin*. This vitamin was at one time called *vitamin B_2*, but the term is now obsolete.

3. *Niacin*. Two chemical substances, *nicotinic acid* and *nicotinamide*, are the principal sources of vitamin activity.

4. *Vitamin B_6*. The principal substance possessing vitamin-B_6 activity is called *pyridoxine*.

5. *Vitamin B_{12}*. The chemical name for this substance is *cyanocobalamin*.

6. *Folic acid*. The chemical substance of which this vitamin is principally composed is called, *pteroylglutamic acid* (PGA).

7. *Pantothenic acid* is a B-vitamin which is widely distributed in foodstuffs.

8. *Biotin* is a vitamin of which very small amounts, even in comparison with other vitamins, are needed.

VITAMIN B$_1$ (THIAMINE, ANEURINE)

1. Vitamin B$_1$ is very soluble in water. It is destroyed by heat and is destroyed particularly readily by heat in the presence of alkali.

2. The function of vitamin B$_1$ in the cells of the body is to form part of one of the *enzymes* by means of which energy is released in a steady, continuous and controlled flow from the carbohydrates of food which constitute one of the principal fuels from which physical energy is derived.

3. Owing to the ready solubility of vitamin B$_1$ in water, it cannot be stored in any large amount in the body. The ill-effects of a dietary deficiency of vitamin B$_1$ consequently become apparent more quickly than would a similar lack of vitamin A, for example.

4. A shortage of vitamin B$_1$ causes the following results:

   (i) Children eating a vitamin B$_1$-deficient diet do not "do well" and their growth is checked.

   (ii) Moderately severe shortage in adults causes fatigueability, apathy and loss of appetite.

   (iii) More prolonged deficiency gives rise to a form of neuritis particularly affecting the legs; the arms may also be involved.

   (iv) The regularity of the heart-beat may also be disturbed.

   (v) Consumption of a poor diet extremely deficient in vitamin B$_1$ results in the disease *beri-beri*. This is a serious disease which may quickly cause death unless it is treated. Although it is seldom seen in Europe, it is common in the Far East where many people live on diets composed principally of white rice from which most of the vitamin B$_1$ has been removed during processing.

FIGURE 10.

Beri-beri due to vitamin B_1-deficiency.

DIETARY SOURCES OF VITAMIN B_1

Vitamin B_1 is widely distributed in foodstuffs but few foods are very rich sources. Among these few are dried yeast, the germ of cereals (in actual fact, there is a structure in seeds called the *scutellum* which is closely associated with the germ; it is the *scutellum* in which the vitamin is most richly concentrated. Its position is shown in Figure 2). Peas, beans and nuts are also rich in vitamin B_1. It is also present in useful amounts in fruit, vegetables and meat, and particularly in lean pork, and in dairy produce.

FOODS DEFICIENT IN VITAMIN B₁

The foods listed below are almost entirely or completely lacking in vitamin B_1. People whose diets contain excessive amounts of these articles consequently run the risk of suffering from nutritional deficiency:

> Sugar
> Starch, cornflower, and highly
>   milled white flour
> White polished rice
> Distilled spirits

Oils and Fats. Since vitamin B_1 is soluble in water, it is not present in oils and fats. However, whereas it is necessary for the proper utilisation of carbohydrates in the body and its absence from sugar and highly milled flour and similar foods is important, fats do not require vitamin B_1 when they are used by the body. The consumption of vitamin B_1-lacking fat does not, in consequence, raise a danger of inducing symptoms of deficiency.

RIBOFLAVIN

1. Riboflavin, like vitamin B_1, is soluble in water. It is a yellow fluorescent substance and its presence contributes to the characteristic yellowy-green colour of whey. Moderate heat, for example, that used in pasteurising or drying milk, does not destroy riboflavin to any significant degree. It is, however, quickly destroyed in strong sunlight.

2. Its function in the cells of the body, again like that of vitamin B_1, is to mediate the release of energy from fuel derived principally from food carbohydrates.

3. A shortage of riboflavin in the diet, if it is sufficiently prolonged, gives rise to the following effects:

(i) The growth of children is checked.

(ii) Soreness and redness of the tongue and lips may occur and cracks may appear at the corners of the mouth.

(iii) The eyes may become bloodshot and small blood vessels may begin to infiltrate the cornea of the eye where it is normally clear and transparent.

DIETARY SOURCES OF RIBOFLAVIN

Riboflavin, again like vitamin B_1, is quite widely distributed in both animal and vegetable foods. Good sources of riboflavin are *milk*, both full-cream and skimmed and both liquid and dried; *liver*, *heart* and *kidney*; and special sources such as *dried yeast* and *yeast extract*. Useful amounts are also contributed by lean meat in general, cheese, eggs and green vegetables. Wholemeal flour and bread contribute riboflavin to the diet but the more highly the wheat is milled the less riboflavin the flour contains.

NIACIN

Consideration of the action of the vitamin, niacin, in the body teaches a lesson in nutrition that applies to many other aspects of the subject. This lesson is that when we are dealing with the functioning of so complex and adaptable an organism as the human being it is very often an over-simplification to say that exactly so much of one specific substance is necessary in the daily diet without which some particular harmful effect will occur. The properties of niacin are these:

1. Niacin, like the other components of the vitamin-B complex, is water soluble.

2. It also, like vitamin B_1 and riboflavin, has a function in the biochemical release of energy in the body.

3. A lack of niacin in the diet produces these results:

   (i)   the growth of children is hindered.

   (ii)   roughening and reddening of the skin occurs, particularly on parts of the body exposed to light.

   (iii)   diarrhoea and other disturbances of digestion occur.

   (iv)   in advanced deficiency, dementia and other mental symptoms may arise.

   (v)   the serious disease, pellagra, which is found in countries where people eat a poor, monotonous diet, particularly if it is largely composed of maize, is primarily due to a deficiency of niacin.

The foods richest in niacin are dried yeast and malt extract. Meat, certain parts of wholemeal flour and notably the bran are good sources and most lightly milled cereals provide useful amounts. But it must be noted that *although pellagra does not occur when adequate amounts of niacin are present in the diet; and although pellagra can be effectively treated by supplying niacin; and although pellagra does occur in some communities when the diet is deficient in niacin, this is not always so.*

It was found that diets in some parts of the world where pellagra was rare contained less niacin than in other areas where it was common. At the same time some foods, of which milk is one, that contain very little niacin, will prevent pellagra. The explanation of these apparent paradoxes was that *tryptophan*, one of the amino acids which forms a component of most animal proteins, may be converted into niacin in the body. It appears that *60 mg. of tryptophan is about equivalent to 1 mg. of niacin.* It follows, therefore, that *harm from a shortage of niacin is only likely to arise when the diet is also deficient in good protein.*

VITAMIN B₆

Although the chemical nature of the group of related substances which possess vitamin B_6-activity is known, and although it is quite well understood that vitamin B_6 plays a part in the conversion of the amino acid, tryptophan, into niacin and in a number of other biochemical mechanisms in which the amino acids of proteins are concerned, it is not clear that adults ever suffer harm from an inadequate supply in their diet. It has been strongly suspected, however, that infants may suffer from certain muscular twitching and convulsive seizures due to vitamin B_6-deficiency if they are receiving a milk diet from which the vitamin has been destroyed by unsatisfactory processing.

The best sources of vitamin B_6 are *meat* and particularly *liver*, *vegetables* and *whole-grain cereals*.

FOLIC ACID

Folic acid is, like vitamin B_{12}, composed of a group of chemically similar substances. The amount of folic acid required from a good diet is not fully understood. The vitamin has, however, been used in medicine in the treatment of anaemia. The best dietary sources of folic acid are *liver, beans and lentils, broccoli, spinach* and other *green leaves*.

Folic acid functions biochemically in the formation of *nucleoproteins*, which are proteins occurring in all cell nuclei. It is, therefore, specially important in the formation of new blood cells.

VITAMIN B₁₂ (CYANOCOBALAMIN)

When it was discovered in 1926 that the incurable disease, pernicious anaemia, could be successfully treated by feeding the patients on substantial amounts of liver, an intensive study was made to discover the component of liver that possessed this anti-pernicious anaemia activity. Twenty-two years later, in 1948, the active substance was identified as vitamin B_{12}. It is a complex chemical compound containing the metal, cobalt.

Vitamin B_{12} is extremely active and very small amounts indeed exert an effect. It is not known how much is needed in the diet of healthy people, but certain extreme vegetarians called Vegans who refuse milk and eggs as well as other animal foods have been found to develop soreness of the mouth and tongue, numbness of the hands and even degeneration of the spinal cord due to vitamin B_{12} deficiency. Vitamin B_{12} also appears to be concerned in the growth of children.

Vitamin B_{12} is present in *liver, kidney, meat* and other animal foods such as *milk, fish* and *eggs*.

PANTOTHENIC ACID

The biochemical function of pantothenic acid in living cells is quite well understood but it is not at all clear to what extent supplies of it are necessary in the diet. It is very widely distributed in foods and is found in specially large amounts in *liver* and *eggs*.

BIOTIN

Biotin, like vitamin B_{12}, is known to be active in extremely small concentrations. Again, a good deal is known about its biochemical function. The point of greatest interest in nutrition is that there is a substance present in raw egg-white which interferes with biotin. Consequently, if *raw* egg-white is eaten in large quantity, biotin cannot function properly and illness occurs. Egg-white does not exert this effect if it is cooked.

THE VITAMIN-B COMPLEX AS A WHOLE

All component members of the vitamin-B complex that we have so far discussed act together in the complex mechanisms of the living cell through which fuel derived from food is caused to release energy and provide the substances by which growth is achieved. So far as diet is concerned, it is quite certain that adequate amounts of *vitamin B_1 and riboflavin must be contributed by foodstuffs*.

It is much more difficult to specify what amounts of the other B-vitamins, *niacin, vitamin B_6, vitamin B_{12}, folic acid, pantothenic acid* and *biotin*, must be supplied in the daily foods we eat. There are several reasons for these doubts, they are:

1. the amount of *niacin* required depends on how much *tryptophan* is also present.

2. it is not clearly understood to what extent we are able to synthesise some of these vitamins in our own bodies.

3. the bacteria present as guests in our intestines are known to synthesise B-vitamins which we can then use to our own advantage.

Our dependence for B-vitamins on the bacteria that we harbour in our gut is at the present time being studied in many universities. Where it has been possible to raise animals from their birth in a sterile environment entirely free from germs, their needs for vitamins from their diet have been greatly modified. Indeed, with some animals it has not been possible under these circumstances to satisfy their nutritional requirement at all even by supplying them with every *known* vitamin. This seems to imply that there are still B-vitamins that are *unknown*.

CHAPTER ELEVEN

VITAMIN C

IT is particularly important for a student of nutrition to have a proper understanding of vitamin C, its chemical properties, and its distribution in foods because it is well within the bounds of possibility for the diet of an infant made up, let us say, of an unduly large proportion of pasteurised milk, or the diet of a middle-aged batchelor comprising an excessive amount of fried sausages, or the diet of an old person living alone and restricted to tea and bread and butter—for all these diets to be seriously lacking in vitamin C and for the people eating them to suffer seriously from the nutritional deficiency.

So far as vitamin A is concerned, the necessary amount for an adequate diet can be obtained from at least four groups of foods: from dairy produce, milk, eggs and the like; from liver and kidney; from fat-containing fish such as herrings; and from green vegetables and carrots with their stocks of vitamin A-active carotene. The B-vitamins as well are widely distributed; in brown bread and many other cereal foods, in potatoes, in dairy produce, in meat—indeed, few foods other than sugar and highly refined cereals are entirely lacking in one or more components of the vitamin B-complex. *Vitamin C, however, is present in significant amounts in only two classes of foods, namely, in fresh vegetables and in fruit and, furthermore, it may be lost or destroyed comparatively easily when these foods are cooked or processed.*

97

THE EFFECTS OF VITAMIN-C DEFICIENCY

Lack of adequate amounts of vitamin C eventually leads to the disease, *scurvy*.

1. Vitamin C-deficiency in Infants

Normal babies are born with sufficient stores of vitamin C to protect them from *scurvy* for about five months. Breast milk will also normally supply enough vitamin C for the baby's needs. However, if a dried-milk formula that is not supplemented with orange juice, added vitamin C (ascorbic acid is its chemical name), or some other source of the vitamin, is fed, the infant will develop scurvy in three months. The following symptoms may occur:

(1) the joints swell and become tender; walking and sitting become painful.
(2) the ribs become sore and breathing may be difficult.
(3) the baby cries when handled.
(4) if the baby has teeth, his gums may bleed.

Administration of vitamin C or foods rich in vitamin C, such as orange juice or rose-hip syrup, produces a rapid cure of the scorbutic symptoms listed above in two or three days.

2. Vitamin C-deficiency in Adults

If an adult eats a diet lacking in vitamin C—that is, one containing no vegetables or fruit—for three or four months, the following symptoms may be expected:

(1) the gums become sore, swollen and spongy; they bleed readily and are easily infected.
(2) thickening and scaliness of the skin occurs.
(3) there is a tendency for slight bleeding to occur at the base of the hairs growing on the legs and thighs; discoloured patches due to small haemorrhages in the skin

may also occur, particularly where there is pressure from clothes.

(4) the healing of wounds and fractures becomes abnormally slow and old wounds may break open.

(5) general weakness and breathlessness is common.

PROPERTIES OF VITAMIN C

1. Vitamin C is soluble in water.

2. The human body is not capable of storing any substantial amount of vitamin C, indeed, large excesses in the diet are almost immediately passed out of the body in the urine. Nevertheless, the symptoms of vitamin-C deficiency described above may not appear until a previously properly fed individual has subsisted on a deficient diet for three or four months.

3. Vitamin C is destroyed by heat. It is consequently lost quite quickly from meals that are kept hot. It is also lost from milk during the heat treatment of pasteurisation or drying.

4. Vitamin C is stable in the plant cells of the green vegetables in which it occurs. When these cells become disrupted, however, either by wilting, or in cooking, or by such mechanical means as grating or mincing, an *enzyme* also contained in the living plant cell comes in contact with the vitamin and destroys it. This cause of loss of vitamin C can be minimised by taking steps to destroy the enzyme itself. This is discussed in Chapter 16.

5. Vitamin C is quite rapidly destroyed in the presence of copper. For this reason it is inadvisable to store vitamin-C-containing foods in copper vessels or to cook them in copper pots. There is a small amount of vitamin C in fresh cows' milk. If milk becomes contaminated by even minute amounts of copper derived from dairy utensils, pasteurising machinery or from water used to wash pails and equipment, the vitamin C will be destroyed.

THE AMOUNTS OF VITAMIN C IN FOODSTUFFS

The vitamin-C content of a number of foods is listed below in Table 12.

TABLE 12

THE VITAMIN C CONTENT OF CERTAIN FOODSTUFFS

	mg. per oz.
Blackcurrants	60
Brussels sprouts	30
Cabbage, watercress, other green vegetables	20
Oranges, lemons, grapefruit	15
Tomato	7
Potatoes	
New	8
October/November	4
December	3
January/February	2
March onwards	1
Lettuce	4
Carrots, onions	3
Apples, plums, pears	1
Fresh milk	0·3

It must again be emphasised that, with the exception of milk which is an unreliable source of small concentrations of the vitamin, *only* fresh fruit and vegetables (including potatoes) supply vitamin C. The other categories of food making up the diet—flour, bread, cereals of all sort; fats and sugar are *entirely devoid of vitamin C*. Meat initially contains traces of vitamin C shortly after the animal from which it is derived is killed, but cooked or processed meats are for all practical purposes *also lacking in vitamin C*. The same applies to fish.

Milk. A breast-fed infant derives the vitamin C it needs from its mother's milk. Cow's milk may also provide a significant contribution of vitamin C when it is introduced into the baby's diet even though, as can be seen from Table 12, the amount of vitamin C in it may only be 0·3 mg. per oz. It is important to remember, however, that pasteurisation, which is an almost essential precaution for maintaining the bacteriological safety of milk handled on a large scale, markedly reduces the amount of vitamin C. More severe processes such as boiling or sterilising will completely destroy vitamin C in milk.

A second factor affecting the vitamin C content of milk is *light*. Milk contains a quite large concentration of the vitamin, riboflavin. This substance in the presence of light destroys vitamin C. If, therefore, a bottle of milk is left for an hour or so in bright morning sunlight on a doorstep, much of the vitamin C in it will be lost.

For these reasons it is wise dietetic practice to give orange juice or some other source of vitamin C at an early age to bottle-fed babies who depend upon milk as a substantial proportion of their food.

* * * *

Potatoes. In the diet of many adults, potatoes provide the most important source of vitamin C throughout the year. Potatoes are commonly eaten every day as part of a normal British diet and are often consumed in substantial quantities. This cannot always be said for green vegetables or fruit. It is important to notice that when potatoes are dug in the autumn they contain twice as much vitamin C as they do in November, and this figure is halved by January or February, and halved again by the spring. It can be seen from these facts that February, March and April are the months to bring out the bottled gooseberries and blackcurrants and to buy imported grapefruit and oranges. This is also the time to serve what greens are available and to put watercress into the sandwiches.

Peas and Beans. Vitamin C is present only in *fresh* vegetables. It follows, therefore, that *green peas* are a useful source. Their average vitamin-C content is about 8 mg. per oz., or approximately the amount present in new potatoes. Similarly, broad beans and string beans or French beans, in which it is actually the immature pod that is eaten, contribute vitamin C to the diet. On the other hand, *dried peas and dried beans, such as haricot beans or baked beans, are entirely devoid of vitamin C.* It is very important, therefore, in ensuring that a diet contains adequate amounts of green vegetables to provide the vitamin C required, to make certain that dried peas and beans have not mistakenly been classified as "vegetables". In this connection it must be remembered that there are several types of peas to be found on the British market which can easily be confused with one another:

1. Fresh peas, frozen peas and canned garden peas may all legitimately be classified as "green vegetables". They all contribute vitamin C to the diet. Broad beans, French beans, string beans and scarlet runners are also vitamin-C containing fresh vegetables.

2. Dried peas and "processed peas", which are dried peas soaked in water and then cooked, often with added colouring matter, and finally canned do not contain any vitamin C. Similarly, dried beans, and canned baked beans which are made with dried beans, contain no vitamin C.

THE FORMATION OF VITAMIN C IN PLANTS

Although dried seeds, including dried peas and beans, do not contain any vitamin C, the vitamin is produced in them when they are sprouted. If, therefore, circumstances arise in which it is not possible to obtain vitamin C from fresh fruit or vegetables, deficiency can be prevented, and an adequate supply obtained if dried peas or grain, such as wheat, barley or rice, is available. By moistening the grain and allowing it to sprout, a source of vitamin C can be produced.

THE SYNTHESIS OF VITAMIN C BY ANIMALS

Human beings require a constant supply of vitamin C in their diet. If it is not available, symptoms of vitamin deficiency will soon occur and after a few months scurvy will develop which, unless relieved, will terminate in death. This need for an outside supply of vitamin C is not shared by all animal species. Guinea-pigs, like man, need vitamin C to protect them against scurvy. Rats on the other hand can make the vitamin for themselves within their own tissues and can in consequence live on a diet from which it is completely lacking.

FACTORS AFFECTING THE BODY'S NEED FOR VITAMIN C

1. **Infection.** People suffering from certain infectious diseases appear to lose vitamin C from their tissues. It is, therefore, reasonable to provide supplementary vitamin C to such patients.

Note. There is no evidence that consumption of *extra vitamin C*, over and above that needed for an adequate diet, provides any protection against common virus infections. *Consequently, there is no basis for recommending orange juice, black-currant puree, or vitamin C pills as a protection against catching colds or influenza.*

2. **Burns.** Burns and other injuries, such as fractures, also lead to a rapid fall in the normal level of vitamin C in the body. Clearly, it is good dietetic practice to insure that adequate supplies of vitamin C are available to patients recovering from these injuries.

3. **Wounds.** Although the precise biochemical function of

vitamin C is not known (unlike the B vitamins, where the bio-chemistry has been quite well worked out) it undoubtedly plays a part in the mechanism by which the healing of wounds occurs. For example, one of the more striking features of acute deficiency—that is to say, of scurvy—is the breaking open of old scars. For this reason, although supplementary vitamin C cannot necessarily be expected to *accelerate* normal wound healing, it is important to ensure that people suffering from wounds are adequately nourished and receive sufficient vitamin C while they are recovering.

SOME PARTICULAR SOURCES OF VITAMIN C

Blackcurrants, followed by the citrus fruits, that is oranges, lemons and grapefruit, are among the richest *common* sources of vitamin C. There are, however, a few other commodities from which the vitamin can be obtained in even higher con-centration. Among these are:

1. Rose Hips

Rose hips may contain up to 700 mg. of vitamin C per oz. compared with the average of 60 mg. per oz. of blackcurrant and 15 mg. per oz. of orange. Different varieties of rose hip may, however, vary widely in the concentration of vitamin C they contain. The average is about 170 mg. per oz. In general, it has been found in Great Britain that hips from roses in Scotland and the north of England contain more vitamin C than those in the south. Few hips can be eaten as such be-cause the fine hairs surrounding the pips irritate the digestive tract. Syrup prepared from rose hips is, however, a useful supplementary source of vitamin C, particularly for children.

2. Green Walnuts

At about the stage of ripeness at which walnuts are nor-mally taken for pickling they contain large quantities of vitamin C often amounting to 500 mg. per oz. If they are prepared by certain domestic recipes, the vitamin-C content of pickled walnuts may be preserved, particularly if they are allowed to retain their green colour. The normal method for commercial pickling usually destroys all the vitamin content.

3. Concentrated Orange Juice

Concentrated orange juice, manufactured under proper conditions, can form a convenient source of vitamin C, particularly for children. It is, however, very important to make sure that a fruit-juice preparation does in fact contain vitamin C before using it as a dietary supplement. Many orange squashes and the like, made primarily as refreshing drinks, may be quite devoid of vitamin content.

CHAPTER TWELVE

VITAMIN D, VITAMIN E AND VITAMIN K

VITAMIN D

WHEREAS the vitamins that we have so far discussed are of importance to adults as well as children, vitamin D is of significance almost exclusively to children. Indeed, it is not entirely certain whether adults require it in their diet at all. *The reason for its special importance to children is that vitamin D is required for the proper growth of bone.* When infants do not obtain adequate supplies, the mineral substances *calcium* and *phosphorus* do not properly combine to form hard, strong bone. The child's growing bones are consequently soft and the disease *rickets* occurs.

Just as vitamin A-activity can be obtained from two sources, namely, the actual vitamin A itself or the vegetable pigment, carotene, which can be converted to vitamin A in the body, so also can vitamin D-activity be acquired in two ways:

(*a*) *Vitamin D* (like vitamin A with which it is, indeed, often associated in foodstuffs) is present in fish oils, dairy produce and a number of other foods.

(*b*) *7-dehydro-cholesterol* is a substance that occurs naturally in the oily component of human skin. This substance is converted into vitamin D by the ultra-violet rays of the sun. Consequently, if the skin of children is exposed to sunlight, vitamin D may be formed in sufficient amount to make them independent of dietary sources. For this reason, rickets has always been a disease of dark, cold climates and is unlikely to occur in the tropics.

Vitamin D (again like vitamin A) is a fat-soluble substance. It is not soluble in water and for this reason once absorbed it is not lost from the body but may be stored in considerable quantities. Advantage is sometimes taken of this property by administering a single massive dose of vitamin D to young children in the autumn to protect them against any possibility of shortage throughout the winter. This method of treatment is known by the German word, *Stosstherapie* ("shock therapy"). Although *Stosstherapie* has its usefulness it is, as a general principle, more desirable to provide a consistent source of vitamin D in the daily diet.

NATURAL SOURCES OF VITAMIN D

A number of the more readily available sources of vitamin D are shown below in Table 13.

TABLE 13

VITAMIN D CONTENT OF CERTAIN FOODSTUFFS :

	*International units** *per oz.*
Tunny-liver oil	up to 7,000,000
Halibut-liver oil	up to 100,000
Cod-liver oil	3,000
Herring, sardine, pilchard, salmon	3,000
Egg-yolk	50
Egg—whole	15
Margarine (vitaminised)	50
Butter	15
Cheese	3
Milk	1

Almost no other classes of food than those shown in the table contain any appreciable amounts of vitamin D at all.

* Vitamin D is coming to be expressed in terms of micrograms of the pure substance, cholecalciferol. 10 I.U. = 0·25 μg cholecalciferol.

There is none in cereal foods, in fruit or vegetables, or in sugar, and only small traces in meat and white fish. Curiously enough, vitamin D is formed in the husks of cocoa-beans through the action of sunlight during the curing process used prior to chocolate manufacture but these do not normally form a source of food.

Note. The common measure of vitamin D-activity, the "international unit", is approximately equal to the activity of 0·025 micrograms of crystalline *calciferol* (the substance produced by irradiating ergosterol).

THE CHEMISTRY OF VITAMIN D

Vitamin D possesses the chemical configuration that causes it to be classified as a member of the group known as *sterols*.

1. Vitamin D_2 (irradiated ergosterol; calciferol)

Vitamin D_2 can be synthesised artificially by irradiating pure ergosterol, a substance derived from yeast. It is also possible to produce some vitamin-D activity in certain foods that do not normally contain it by subjecting them to ultra-violet irradiation. This practice is not much done any more since it raises the possibility of raising the vitamin-D content of a diet to undesirably high levels. For certain species of animals, including children, pigs, calves and rats, vitamin D_2 appears to be as effective as vitamin D_3. However, it is less potent for preventing rickets in poultry, which may readily suffer from this disease if they are improperly fed.

2. Vitamin D_3 (found naturally in cod-liver oil, dairy produce etc.)

Vitamin D_3, which, like vitamin D_2, can also be produced artifically, appears to possess equal anti-rachitic activity for poultry and for the other species previously listed, including infants.

HARMFUL RESULTS FROM TOO MUCH VITAMIN D

Overdosing with concentrates of vitamin D or the consumption, unawares, of items of food to which vitamin D has been added or in which it has been induced by unnecessary irradiation can result in a number of harmful results. Two of these are described below.

(i) *Idiopathic hypercalcaemia* in infants. The babies suffer from loss of appetite, vomiting, wasting and constipation.

(ii) More serious symptoms and even death have been recorded where excessively large amounts of vitamin D have been consumed.

INDICATIONS OF VITAMIN D DEFICIENCY

1. Vitamin D is essential to protect infants who live in temperate climates from *rickets*.

2. Since a rickety baby's ribs may soften and its muscles become flabby, its breathing may be hampered and it may, in consequence, be predisposed to *respiratory disease*.

3. Vitamin D is concerned with the proper formation of *teeth* as well as bones. Deficiency, either in the diet of the infant or of the expectant mother, may increase the likelihood of the baby's teeth decaying.

4. *Osteomalacia* is a rare disease affecting the bones of adults and particularly women who have nursed their babies for prolonged periods while themselves eating a very inadequate diet. It is considered to be the adult counterpart of rickets.

VITAMIN E (TOCOPHEROL)

Vitamin E is a fat soluble substance the chemical nature of which has been fully elucidated. There are, in fact, four different substances of quite similar chemical structure all of which exert vitamin-E activity. They are distinguished by the Greek letters, alpha, beta, gamma and delta. The first of these, *alpha tocopherol* as it is called, is somewhat more potent than the others, and is the form in which vitamin E is synthesised commercially.

THE DISTRIBUTION OF VITAMIN E IN FOODS

Vitamin E is present in almost all foods. It is present in highest concentration in the fatty component of cereal grain and wheat-germ oil is a particularly active source. It is also present in the fatty fraction of leaves and in eggs. In contrast, animal fats are comparatively poor sources of the vitamin.

THE ACTION OF VITAMIN E

1. Although vitamin E is known to occur in human tissues and although it is almost certain that it plays a part in the functioning of healthy cells, *it is not at all certain that a supply of vitamin E in the human diet is strictly necessary*. Up till the present, ill-health due to shortage of vitamin E has never been proved to occur, nor have any symptoms of malnutrition ever been cured by administering vitamin E.

2. The reasons why it is useful for students of nutrition to know about vitamin E are:

(*a*) because a number of animals of different species, including cattle and sheep, goats, rabbits, hamsters and rats, suffer severely from vitamin E-deficiency, as is described below. It is possible, therefore, that there may be circumstances, as yet unknown, when lack of vitamin E may be harmful to human welfare also.

(*b*) vitamin E in foods is known to possess the ability to protect natural fats, and vitamin A in them, from the destructive effect of oxygen. By virtue of this property, it is called an *anti-oxidant*.

Vitamin E as an anti-oxidant

It may well be that the ability of vitamin E to protect fats and such substances as vitamin A that are associated with them from oxidation is its principal useful function for human diets. As the main natural anti-oxidant in foods, it protects fats from rancidity. The fact that under normal circumstances additional vitamin E has not been found to improve human diets and lack of vitamin E has not been implicated with any specific signs or symptoms of malnutrition may be because human beings are normally capable of producing in their own tissues enough of the vitamin for their needs. Other animals, on the contrary, need to obtain adequate supplies in their diet. It has been suggested that the basic function of vitamin E in animal biology is to act as an anti-oxidant in living cells and to prevent the oxidation of fuel in the muscles (by which life is made to "go") from speeding up too fast and thus causing wear and tear and hence degeneration of the muscle.

VITAMIN E DEFICIENCY IN ANIMALS

1. *Calves, sheep, goats, hamsters, rabbits and guinea pigs.* A dietary deficiency of vitamin E causes severe degeneration of the principal muscles to develop.

2. *Cattle.* Lack of vitamin E in cattle may lead to death from a particular form of heart disease.

3. *Poultry.* The eggs from vitamin E-deficient hens do not hatch properly and the chicks that do survive may die of brain-injury and an accumulation of fluid in their tissues.

4. *Rats.* Female rats deficient in vitamin E fail to produce their litters. Male rats also become sterile. It is this phenomenon that led to vitamin E being called at one time the "anti-sterility" vitamin.

111

VITAMIN K

Vitamin K is another fat-soluble vitamin. Its chemical nature is known and it is quite readily synthesised. The synthetic material is called *menaphthene* in Great Britain and *menadione* in the United States. It is available as the pure substance or as tablets. There are, in fact, two quite similar active substances, often called vitamin K_1, which is naturally present in leafy vegetables, and vitamin K_2, which is synthesised by micro-organisms.

Vitamin K is not usually of direct practical significance to the nutritionist concerned with the diets of healthy people but its mode of action is nevertheless of great interest.

THE FUNCTION OF VITAMIN K IN THE BODY

Vitamin K is necessary for the formation in the liver of a substance called *prothrombin* which is one of the materials which brings about the clotting of blood following an injury. Normal healthy people do not need to obtain any supply of vitamin K in their food. *Enough vitamin K for the body's needs is synthesised by the bacteria which form the normal population of the intestines.*

CLASSES OF PEOPLE WHO REQUIRE SUPPLEMENTARY SUPPLIES OF VITAMIN K

1. Infants

A new-born infant has no bacteria in its intestines and it is usually fed on foods that are relatively free from bacterial infection. Furthermore, human milk and clean cow's milk are very poor sources of the vitamin. Following from this, it is found that infants in their first week of life have less prothrombin in their blood than they do in later life. In a small number of infants, amounting to less than one per cent, bleeding may occur. Although it is not certain that this is due to a direct deficiency of vitamin K, it is considered prudent practice in these cases to administer vitamin K. The most convenient way to do this is in the form of a tablet. For the most part, normal infants quickly establish a bacterial colony in their intestine and hence become independent of outside sources of vitamin K.

2. Patients with Obstructive Jaundice

The salts naturally occurring in *bile* (see Chapter 13) are essential for the absorption of vitamin K. These salts are lacking in people suffering from obstructive jaundice. The use of vitamin K in the treatment of such patients, particularly when an operation is necessary, has proved to be very valuable.

SOURCES OF VITAMIN K

1. Foodstuffs

Vitamin K is quite widely distributed in foods. Besides occurring in green vegetables, it is also present in tomatoes, cauliflowers, egg yolk and liver. Among less common sources are soya-bean oil and pine needles.

2. Bacterial Synthesis

Vitamin K, as has already been said, is produced by the bacteria in our intestines. It is also produced, however, by the bacteria that cause food to go bad. One of the first good sources of vitamin K to be discovered was putrid fish meal.

*   *   *   *

It is worth emphasising, once more, that nutrition is a complex science and that the precise nutritional composition necessary for a good diet, although it can be set out in considerable detail, cannot be stated in full. There must always be a balance between the nature of the foods providing the nutrients, the physiological efficiency of the individual eating the diet, and the surroundings in which he exists, of which the bacteria living within him in his digestive tract comprise an important factor.

CHAPTER THIRTEEN

THE DIGESTION AND ABSORPTION OF FOOD

THE human body is made up of a multitude of living cells. It is the function of food to keep these cells alive and "going". When we define food, therefore, as something which supplies *the body* with (i) energy, (ii) substances for making it grow and (iii) materials that regulate its functions, it is clear that food can do none of these things *unless it is absorbed into the cells of which the body is composed*.

When a piece of bread is first put into a person's mouth, it has not exerted any of the properties of food and it can be spat out. Indeed, substances can travel farther into the body than the mouth without necessarily being *absorbed*. For example, even after poison has reached the stomach, it can be recovered again if an emetic is given quickly enough *before absorption has occurred*. This leads to two propositions:

1. As long as nutrients remain in the digestive tract, they are not yet *in* the body's cells and cannot exert their functions as the essential components of food.

2. On the other hand, if food has exerted its function of supplying energy, or growth, or regulation, it must have been *absorbed* into the body's cells.

It is important for the student of nutrition to understand the nature of the living body. This consists of two components:

1. **The Living Tissues of the Body.** This comprises the head and trunk, the limbs, the skeleton, the skin, the blood system and, in fact, all the parts through which blood flows.

2. **The digestive tract.**   Within the structure of the living tissues there lies what is, in spite of many elaborations, a tube open at both ends.   As long as food is within this tube, *it is still outside the body*.   It is only when the digested food has "soaked" through the moist sides of the digestive tract into the blood that circulates on the other side that it can be said to be *inside* the body.

This leads to two definitions:

Digestion.   Most ordinary foodstuffs cannot pass through the walls of the digestive tract *into* the body itself in the form in which they are eaten.   Before this can happen, they must be broken down into their component nutrients and these nutrients must themselves often be split into small fragments through the action of a series of *enzymes* in the *digestive juices*.

Absorption.   The process by which separate nutrients or their fragments are passed *through* the walls of the digestive tract into the blood is *absorption*.   Only after *absorption* has taken place can the body obtain benefit from food.

The process of digestion and absorption takes place in the digestive tract which starts at the mouth and extends, *via* the stomach, small intestine, and the large intestine to the rectum, from which indigestible residues are finally excreted from the body.   A diagram of this long and convoluted system of tubes in shown in Figure 11.

THE PROCESS OF DIGESTION

1. The Mouth

(*a*) The main process occurring in the mouth is the mechanical breaking down of food by chewing which enables the *digestive enzymes*, which subsequently bring

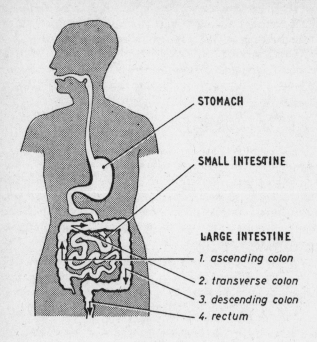

FIGURE 11.
A diagram of the digestive tract.

about the chemical subdivision of the food into its components, to penetrate and do their work. The basic purpose of these enzymes is to make the food components dissolve in water. Solid particles cannot be absorbed.

(b) The chewed-up food is mixed with *saliva* which breaks down a small amount of cooked *starch* into the soluble sugar, *maltose*.

2. The Stomach

(a) More mixing and mechanical breakdown take place in the stomach, although, as can be felt by people who "bolt" their food, the stomach is less efficient than the mouth, teeth and jaws for this purpose.

(b) In the stomach, the food is mixed with between 2 and 3 quarts of *gastric juice* which is produced there each day by a normal adult. Gastric juice contains an enzyme, *pepsin*, in a quite strong solution of 0·2–0·4% *hydrochloric acid* and exerts the following effect on food:

(i) The complex amino-acid structure of proteins is partly broken down.

(ii) Milk is curdled in preparation for the later stages of digestion.

3. The Small Intestine

(a) *Starch* is broken down into the simple, soluble sugar, *glucose*, in the small intestine.

(b) *Proteins*, already partially digested in the stomach, are divided into their amino-acid units.

(c) *Fats* are emulsified, in much the same way that cream is mingled with the other constituents of homogenised milk, so that it forms what almost amounts to a watery solution.

4. The Large Intenstine

(a) *Cellulose* and *hemi-cellulose*, of which the outer husks of beans and cereal grains and the tougher parts of vegetables are composed, may be attacked by the bacteria that live in the large intestine. While this gives the bacteria the sustenance they need, it may at the same time make available to the human host a portion of the substance so attacked.

(b) *Vitamins*. As has already been said, the bacteria in the large intestine may synthesise, for their own purposes, vitamins which may then be of use to the individual in whose intestine they are. This is not strictly digestion but it is nevertheless an aspect of nutrition arising from the action of the large intestine.

THE PROCESS OF ABSORPTION

1. **The Mouth.** Not very much of the food that is eaten is absorbed through the tongue or the lining of the inside of the mouth. Certain soluble nutrients, including such substances as salt, sugar (whether table sugar [sucrose] or glucose) and certain soluble drugs as well, can be absorbed in the mouth.

2. **The Stomach.** Although the stomach is to a large extent a compartment in which foodstuffs are mixed with gastric juice in preparation for subsequent absorption in the further parts of the digestive tract, a number of substances pass into the bloodstream through its lining. These are:

(a) Alcohol.

(b) Sugar.

(c) Salt and other water-soluble minerals.

(d) Water-soluble vitamins, i.e. B-vitamins, and vitamin C.

(e) Although it is not strictly a nutrient, it should be noted that water itself is absorbed into the blood through the lining of the stomach.

3. **The Small Intestine.** This is where the major part of the process of absorption takes place. The digestion of the three principal categories of nutrients is completed in the small intestine and it is there that they are absorbed. The list of food components absorbed through the small intestine thus becomes:

(*a*) Carbohydrate.

(*b*) Protein.

(*c*) Fat.

(*d*) Mineral substances.

(*e*) Vitamins, both water-soluble and fat-soluble.

(*f*) Water.

4. **The Large Intestine.** Very little absorption takes place through the large intestine since most of the material capable of absorption has already been absorbed in earlier sections of the digestive tract. Two items are, however, absorbed into the body at this stage.

(*a*) Vitamins of the B-group and possibly others synthesised by micro-organisms present in the large intestine.

(*b*) One of the principal functions of the large intestine is the absorption of *water* from the faeces so that too much moisture will not be lost from the body when the stools are passed.

THE PROCESS OF EATING

1. **Appetite.** Appetite is a more complicated phenomenon than it may at first sight appear. As a general rule, the appetite is a remarkably accurate regulator of the body's needs for food, but as is very obvious on occasion this is not always so. For example, people may eat because they are bored or unhappy and, on the other hand, they may refuse food when they are angry, frightened or in love even when it can be demonstrated that they have need for it.

There are three main factors that regulate appetite:

(*a*) *Chemical regulation.* The relative concentration of glucose in the arteries and veins has a direct effect on appetite.

119

Immediately after a meal the glucose level in the arterial blood is relatively high. As time passes, it gradually falls and as it does so the sensation of hunger is aroused.

(*b*) *Nervous stimuli.* The central nervous system, of which the brain is the co-ordinating organ, has a controlling effect on appetite. We have already referred to the influence of the emotions on appetite. Habit and custom, which are themselves attitudes of mind, clearly play a part as well. Psychological disease may also affect appetite. The most obvious effect of the mind on appetite is that the thought, sight or smell of food, transmitted by the higher centres of the brain, or by the optic or the olfactory nerves, can cause saliva to flow into the mouth and gastric juice into the stomach.

(*c*) *The hypothalamous.* This is a small organ situated at the base of the brain. It is now clear that it has a profound effect on appetite. In most people its influence is such that their appetite tallies with their needs; in certain individuals, however, satisfaction of appetite, as regulated by the hypothalamous, occurs at a point when more food has been eaten than is necessary for the body's requirements. When this is so, obesity occurs.

2. **Food in the Stomach.** The food, mixed with saliva, passes down the *oesophagus* into the stomach. Digestion in the stomach may take from 2 to 4 hours before the food is reduced to a semi-liquid state. It is then squirted through the lower end of the stomach into the small intestine.

3. **Passage Through the Small Intestine.** The now partially digested food is passed through the small intestine, which is about 20 ft. long and 1 in. in diameter, by rhythmic muscular contractions. Absorption of nutrients occurs continuously throughout the length of the intestine, which comprises three parts:

(a) The first 12 in. or so, the *duodenum*, where intestinal juices are introduced. ("Duodecem" is Latin for 12.)

(b) The *jejunum* comprises the next 9 ft. This section is normally found empty after death, hence the name derived from "jejunus", the Latin for empty.

(c) The *ileum* is the last 9 or 10 ft. of the small intestine.

4. **Passage Through the Large Intestine.** The residues of food remaining unabsorbed together with the mixture of unused digestive juices pass out of the ileum into the large intestine. This is a tube, larger in diameter than the small intestine but only about 5 ft. long. At first the faecal residues travel *upwards* through that part of the intestine on the right side of the abdomen called the *ascending colon*. The large intestine then passes across the abdomen to the left side. This is called the *tranverse colon*. The last main part of the intestine travels down the left side of the abdomen and is called the *descending colon*. The faeces are finally expelled through the *anus*. It is quite normal in healthy people for the faecal remains of a meal to leave the body 24 hours or more after the meal was eaten.

THE ABSORPTION OF WATER

1. It will be recalled that one of the fundamental principles of physiology is that the body must at all times maintain constant conditions within itself. When water is drunk, it is quickly absorbed into the bloodstream. If it were allowed to remain it would, of course, dilute the blood. The body possesses a delicate mechanism by which any excess of water that may be absorbed is quickly excreted.

2. The *kidneys* are the organs that automatically control the water-equilibrium of the blood. The control exerted by the kidneys is so sensitive that within an hour of drinking in excess of the body's needs, the surplus water is excreted as urine.

DIGESTIBILITY

When a normal mixed diet is eaten by a healthy person with good teeth, the nutrients in the food are almost completely digested. The figures that normally apply are as follows:

Carbohydrates	98%	digestible
Fat	95%	,,
Protein	92%	,,

The speed of digestion, which may also be called "ease" of digestion, is affected by a number of factors. Three of these are:

(a) *Fat.* Fat eaten with other foods possesses the power of delaying the passage of those foods through the stomach. This has two effects, on the one hand it renders fatty food slower—or, as it is usually put, "more difficult"—to digest. On the other hand, fat, by delaying the emptying of the stomach at the same time delays the return of hunger. Fats are for this reason said to possess a high *satiety value.*

(b) *Flavour, aroma and appearance.* Attractive, tasty meals will cause the saliva and gastric juice to flow. That is to say, they make one's mouth water. For this reason their digestion is facilitated. But again it is important to remember two things:

(i) Because a steaming plate of roast pork, rich in fat, makes the digestive juices flow and is then itself more readily digested than it would be had it been half cold on a chipped plate, this does not make it more digestible than a piece of stale dry bread. Bread is, in fact, readily digested.

(ii) The fact that certain foods may be strongly disliked does not to any marked degree detract from their digestibility *provided that they are eaten.* The principal nutritional importance of attractiveness in food is that people are caused to eat it.

(c) *Indigestible residues.* Some foods contain residues which are, in fact, incapable of being digested. Green vegetables may contain fibrous portions composed in part of *cellulose* which cannot be digested. As has already been mentioned, peas and beans may contain *hemi-cellulose* which can only be digested to a small degree. Gristle and connective tissue of meat may be highly resistant to digestion and inadequately cooked potatoes and cereals may contain unbroken plant cells which protect the starch granules inside them and may prevent their digestion.

CHAPTER FOURTEEN

NUTRITIONAL REQUIREMENTS

IN the chapters of this book up to this point we have discussed each of the various separate nutrients which are required for an adequate diet. *This is the first lesson of nutrition: that food must provide all the different nutrients whose function has so far been described*. We now turn to a different but equally important aspect of the subject. *This second lesson is that each of the diverse nutrients necessary for a balanced diet must be present in the appropriate amount*.

Nutrition is a quantitative science. For health and efficiency an individual must eat *sufficient* of all the nutrients so far discussed. This requires that the student of nutrition should know (*a*) the composition of the different foods of which the diet is composed in terms of calories, protein, fat, minerals and vitamins and also (*b*) the amounts of each nutrient necessary. By using the available knowledge of food composition it is possible to design an adequate diet in an almost infinitely large number of ways and thus satisfy the tastes and customs of the people for whom the diet is intended and at the same time take advantage of the available food supplies.

RECOMMENDED DAILY DIETARY ALLOWANCES

The figures shown below in Table 14 are the allowances recommended by the British Department of Health and Social Security in 1969. A number of groups of experts in other countries, notably the United States, India, Canada and elsewhere, have put together similar tables of recommen-

TABLE 14
RECOMMENDED DAILY INTAKES OF ENERGY AND NUTRIENTS FOR THE UK

(a) Age range	Occupational category	(c) Body weight kg	(d) Energy kcal	(d) Energy MJ	(f) Protein g	(g) Thiamine mg	Riboflavine mg	Nicotinic acid mg equivalents	Ascorbic acid mg	Vitamin A (i) μg retinol equivalents	Vitamin D (j) μg cholecalciferol	Calcium mg	Iron mg
BOYS AND GIRLS												(l)	(l)
0 up to 1 year (b)		7.3	800	3.3	20	0.3	0.6	5	15	450	10	600	6
1 up to 2 years		11.4	1200	5.0	30	0.5	0.6	7	20	300	10	500	7
2 up to 3 years		13.5	1400	5.9	35	0.6	0.7	8	20	300	10	500	7
3 up to 5 years		16.5	1600	6.7	40	0.6	0.8	9	20	300	10	500	8
5 up to 7 years		20.5	1800	7.5	45	0.7	0.9	10	20	300	2.5	500	8
7 up to 9 years		25.1	2100	8.8	53	0.8	1.0	11	20	400	2.5	500	10
BOYS													
9 up to 12 years		31.9	2500	10.5	63	1.0	1.2	14	25	575	2.5	700	13
12 up to 15 years		45.5	2800	11.7	70	1.1	1.4	16	25	725	2.5	700	14
15 up to 18 years		61.0	3000	12.6	75	1.2	1.7	19	30	750	2.5	600	15
GIRLS													
9 up to 12 years		33.0	2300	9.6	58	0.9	1.2	13	25	575	2.5	700	13
12 up to 15 years		48.6	2300	9.6	58	0.9	1.4	16	25	725	2.5	700	14
15 up to 18 years		56.1	2300	9.6	58	0.9	1.4	16	30	750	2.5	600	15
MEN													
18 up to 35 years	Sedentary	65	2700	11.3	68	1.1	1.7	18	30	750	2.5	500	10
	Moderately active		3000	12.6	75	1.2	1.7	18	30	750	2.5	500	10
	Very active		3600	15.1	90	1.4	1.7	18	30	750	2.5	500	10
35 up to 65 years	Sedentary	65	2600	10.9	65	1.0	1.7	18	30	750	2.5	500	10
	Moderately active		2900	12.1	73	1.2	1.7	18	30	750	2.5	500	10
	Very active		3600	15.1	90	1.4	1.7	18	30	750	2.5	500	10
65 up to 75 years	} Assuming a sedentary life	63	2350	9.8	59	0.9	1.7	18	30	750	2.5	500	10
75 and over		63	2100	8.8	53	0.8	1.7	18	30	750	2.5	500	10
WOMEN													
18 up to 55 years	Most occupations	55	2200	9.2	55	0.9	1.3	15	30	750	2.5	500	12
	Very active		2500	10.5	63	1.0	1.3	15	30	750	2.5	500	12
55 up to 75 years	} Assuming a sedentary life	53	2050	8.6	51	0.8	1.3	15	30	750	2.5	500	10
75 and over		53	1900	8.0	48	0.7	1.3	15	30	750	2.5	500	10
Pregnancy, 2nd and 3rd trimester			2400	10.0	60	1.0	1.6	18	60	750	10	1200 (m)	15
Lactation			2700	11.3	68	1.1	1.8	21	60	1200	10	1200	15

Footnotes to Table 14

(a) The ages are from one birthday to another: e.g. 9 up to 12 is from the 9th up to, but not including, the 12th birthday. The figures in the Table in general refer to the mid-point of the ranges though those for the range 18 up to 35 refer to the age 25 years, and for the range 18 up to 55, to 35 years of age.

(b) Average figures relating to the first year of life. Energy and minimum protein requirements in terms of the four trimesters are given in Tables 2 and 3 respectively.

(c) The body weights of children and adolescents are averages and relate to London in 1965. (Taken from Tanner, Whitehouse & Takaishi, 1966; Tables IV A and IV B, 50th centile). The body weights of adults do not represent average values; they are those of the FAO (1957) reference man and woman, with a nominal reduction for the elderly.

(d) Megajoules (10⁶ joules). Calculated from the relation 1 kilocalorie = 4.186 kilojoules, and rounded to 1 decimal place.

(f) Recommended intakes calculated as providing 10 per cent of energy requirements (see paragraph 64). Minimum protein requirements given in Table 3.

(g) The figures, calculated from energy requirements and the recommended intake of thiamine of 0.4 mg/1000 kcal, relate to groups of individuals.

(i) 1 retinol equivalent = 1 μg retinol or 6 μg β-carotene or 12 μg other biologically active carotenoids.

(j) No dietary source may be necessary for those adequately exposed to sunlight, but the requirement for the housebound may be greater than that recommended.

(k) For all three trimesters.

(l) These figures apply to infants who are not breast fed. Infants who are entirely breast fed receive smaller quantities; these are adequate since absorption from breast milk is higher.

(m) For the third trimester only.

(Department of Health and Social Security, Rep. 120, H.M.S.O., 1969.)

dations each of which has differed to a minor degree from the other. It is clear, however, that if the amounts of nutrients shown in the table are consumed, complete dietary health will be maintained in the different types of people eating them and no further addition of nutrients would produce any improvement in health.

THE EFFECT OF VARIATION FROM THE IDEAL NUTRITIONAL INTAKE

The recommended allowances of the different nutrients shown in Table 14 are *estimates* for *average* members of the different categories of people described and the figures apply to normal individuals living in a temperate climate in a country like Great Britain. These values are targets and it is important to understand the degree of harm likely to occur if the recommended allowance of any particular nutrient is not available.

1. **Calories.** As was described in Chapter 5, it is the amount of physical work done that most directly affects the number of calories required. If a man is doing hard physical work and does not obtain his calorific needs he will first of all become *hungry*. Should the food shortage continue he will lose weight. But besides being dependent on work, the calorie need is also related to body weight. A big man needs more calories than a small one. Consequently, when a man has lost weight, his calorie *requirement* is less. A population receiving too little to eat will become thin but may be able to continue indefinitely provided the calorie deficiency is not too severe. This is, in fact, the mechanism by which the body protects itself against harm from food shortage. It is nevertheless true that prolonged calorie deficiency will harmfully affect bodily vigour.

2. **Protein.** It can be seen from Table 14 that the requirement for protein is increased:

(a) For rapidly growing boys and girls of 11–14 years.

(b) For adolescents between 15 and 19 years, particularly boys.

(c) For pregnant women and nursing mothers.

Very heavy workers who obtain their full calorie requirement from a normal mixed diet will readily obtain the target figures for protein set down in the table. For children and mothers, it is not only important to consider the total amount of protein but also its *amino-acid composition*. Although it is possible for experts in protein chemistry to design an appropriate mixture of cereal and vegetable protein to satisfy the needs of these groups, it is most satisfactory in practice where food supplies are available to ensure that an adequate proportion of the total protein is derived from animal food, for example, milk, meat, eggs or fish. The following proportions of animal protein are commonly recommended:

	Proportion of total protein to be from animal sources
	%
Young children	60–100%
Children of school age	55– 60%
Adolescents	35– 55%
Expectant mothers	45– 55%
Nursing mothers	50– 75%

In many parts of the world infants and young children are fed on cereal gruels; the disease, *Kwashiorkor*, due to protein malnutrition arising from this practice is one of the most widespread and damaging deficiency diseases of the twentieth century.

3. **Fat.** It will be noticed that no fixed amount of fat is set down in Table 14 as a recommended allowance for nutritional well-being. Although it is almost certain that a small amount of fat is a necessary nutritional requirement, it is probable that the strictly nutritional need is quite small. In actual practice, however, the most important nutritional functions of fat are:

(a) *To provide calories in a concentrated form.* It will be remembered that 1 oz. of fat provides 252 calories compared with 73 from 1 oz. of dry bread and 21 from 1 oz. of boiled potato.

(b) *To make other foods palatable.* In many communities, including that of Great Britain, a diet containing only a small amount of fat is considered unpalatable and, in consequence, it may not be eaten willingly. It is worth remembering that malnutrition may arise from the refusal to eat unattractive foods as well as from the unavailability of the appropriate foods.

It is often considered a useful guiding principle to include sufficient fat, in a diet of 3000 calories or less, to provide 25% of the total calories. For workers needing more than 3000 calories a day, if 30% is provided by fat, the diet need not be too bulky. These proportions are designed rather for convenience and palatability than to fulfil a definite physiological requirement. It is also important to remember that an unduly *high* fat consumption, particularly by middle-aged men, has been found to be associated with an increased susceptibility to coronary heart disease. This point was discussed in Chapter 3.

4. **Calcium.** It is particularly important that the recommended allowances of calcium for expectant and nursing mothers should be attained since they are actively concerned with the laying down of calcium in developing teeth and bones. Similarly, an adequate supply of calcium is needed by growing children. For this reason, milk is a valuable food for these groups. They also need to obtain the amounts of vitamin D, or its equivalent in the form of plenty of sunshine. Although scientific opinion in Western countries favours the consumption by adults of 0·8 g. of calcium daily, as set down in Table 14, it is known that there are populations who obtain less calcium over prolonged periods and who suffer no detectable harm.

5. **Iron.** It is difficult to say how essential it is for men to obtain the 12 mg. of iron recommended each day. Iron is only absorbed by the body when it is needed. Deficiency of iron is one cause of anaemia, a condition in which there is a shortage of the red blood pigment, haemoglobin, which is an iron-containing substance. *Women have a more urgent need for iron than men* because they suffer from a periodical loss of blood. For women, therefore, there may be little or no margin below the recommended dietary intake of 12 mg. of iron.

6. **Vitamin A.** It can be seen from the figures in Table 14 that nursing mothers have need for the highest intake of vitamin A in their diet if the optimum health of their babies and themselves is to be maintained. As was described in Chapter 9, substantial stores of vitamin A may be carried in the liver so that a temporary deficiency in the diet will not be harmful provided the foods previously eaten contained adequate amounts.

It will also be seen that the recommended allowance for adults of 750 μg. retinol equivalents is the amount suggested from a mixed diet containing vitamin A derived from animal foods—butter, eggs, liver, fish and fish oils—as well as from green vegetables and carrots containing vitamin A-active carotene. The recommended intake is probably an upper figure certain to ensure optimum nutrition under the most unfavourable circumstances likely to be met among normal individuals. It also includes some margin of insurance. A minimum intake sufficient merely to ensure freedom from symptoms of vitamin A-deficiency might be, say, 500 μg. daily. Since the vitamin A-activity from carotene is less effective than the activity from vitamin A itself, a daily minimum even less than 500 μg. might be enough provided it was all derived from animal sources.

7. **Vitamin B$_1$.** The recommended allowances of vitamin B$_1$ provide a handsome margin for most ordinary people. A safe *minimum* for protection against symptoms of deficiency

would be about half the figures listed. In considering the physiological need for vitamin B_1 it is important to remember that its function is in the utilisation of carbohydrate. Consequently, when a heavy worker makes up his extra calories by eating more sugar and starchy foods, his needs for vitamin B_1 are increased accordingly. It is because an increase in calorie requirement almost always *is* accompanied by an increased consumption of carbohydrate that the recommended allowances of vitamin B_1 are shown as increasing in parallel. However, the utilisation of *fat* by the body does not involve vitamin B_1. If, therefore, a hard worker increases his calorie intake by raising his consumption of fat, his need for vitamin B_1 will *not* increase correspondingly.

8. **Riboflavin.** Although riboflavin is known to be concerned with the production of energy in the body, it has not been easy to demonstrate that people who live energetic lives, and who consequently have increased calorie demands, do actually benefit from an increased intake of riboflavin as recommended in Table 14. For these groups, at least, a supply of, say, half the recommended amounts would not be harmful, at least for a very long time.

9. **Niacin.** As was described in Chapter 10, the requirement for niacin is related to the amount of the amino acid, *tryptophane*, in the diet. Under normal circumstances, when Western diets are being eaten, harmful shortage of niacin is very unlikely. Demonstrable niacin deficiency is, indeed, rarely seen unless a substantial amount of maize is included in the diet.

10. **Vitamin C.** Not long ago it was thought that substantially more than 20 mg. of vitamin C daily was required by an adult. This figure now recommended in Table 14 is a revision of a higher recommendation and is probably the minimum safe value for a healthy diet. Another reason why a prudent nutritionist would take steps to ensure that this is the target is that vitamin C is easily lost in wilted vegetable or destroyed by over-cooking or keeping foods hot.

A GOOD MIXED DIET

It is the responsibility of the nutritionist to ensure that the different groups of people in any community—the sedentary people, the heavy workers, the children and the mothers—obtain the appropriate amounts of each of the various nutrients necessary for the health of the body. This can be done by measurement and calculation as described in later chapters. It can be attained in a large number of ways with a wide variety of different foods to suit different tastes and to conform to different customs. But besides the precise assessment of calories, protein, vitamins and minerals, a more rapid method that gives at least a first approximation in the assessment of a good diet is to ensure that the daily food supply always contains representatives of each of the following food groups:

1. The *"body-building" foods*   (i) Meat, fish, eggs, poultry, dried peas and beans.

                                   (ii) Milk, cheese.

2. The *"protective" foods*   (iii) Vegetables, potatoes, fruit.

                                   (iv) Butter, vitaminised margarine.

3. The *"fuel" foods*   (v) Bread, flour, cereals.

The nutritional requirements must be assessed in terms of the quantities of nutrients set out in Table 14, but a good diet must interpret these in terms of food. When it does so, it may also supply the numerous other nutrients that are known but whose quantitative demands have not yet been established. We hope that it will also provide as well the other nutrients that are as yet only suspected and that have not so far been identified.

CHAPTER FIFTEEN

THE COMPOSITION OF FOOD

THE average composition of a list of various foodstuffs is given in the table at the end of this book. It must always be remembered, however, that the actual specimen of food, bought at a particular shop, cooked in a particular kitchen, and eaten from a particular plate may differ quite markedly in composition from the *average* values for the type of food of which it is a portion. For example, it may be true that 1 oz. of mutton, on average, contains 8·8 grams of fat and provides 94 calories, as is set down in the table. On the other hand, one particular individual may obtain from the butcher mutton that is a great deal more fatty than the average and consequently provides many more calories, whereas another person, whose diet is under review, may never eat any mutton fat at all. It follows, therefore, that research workers carrying out precise scientific studies need to analyse duplicates of everything that is eaten and drunk. The student of nutrition, however, can avoid the more serious errors and at the same time use food tables if he knows something of the chemical make-up of the different types of food.

1. Cereals

The main component of all the common cereals is the carbohydrate, *starch*. It is this starch that contributes the major proportion of the calories of the daily diet. The different structures of wheat, rice, oats, barley, rye and maize are shown in Figure 12. The principal differences in composition are listed in Table 15.

TABLE 15

THE COMPOSITION OF DIFFERENT CEREAL GRAINS
(per oz)

	Calories	Protein g.	Fat g.	Carbohydrate g.	Calcium mg.	Iron m.g.	Vitamin A i.u.	Vitamin B1 m.g.	Riboflavin mg.	Niacin mg.	Vitamin C mg.
Wheat, wholemeal	95	3·9	0·9	17·4	10	1·0	nil	0·12	0·06	0·8	nil
Rice, white	99	1·8	0·3	22·2	1	0·1	nil	0·02	0·02	0·3	nil
Maize, wholemeal	99	2·7	1·7	14·4	4	1·4	0–100	0·09	0·04	0·2	nil
Barley, pearl	97	2·2	0·5	20·8	3	0·2	nil	0·03	0·01	0·7	nil
Oats, oatmeal	111	3·4	2·5	18·6	16	1·2	nil	0·13	0·04	0·3	nil
Rye	89	3·0	0·6	24·2	14	0·9	nil	0·08	0·03	0·3	nil

(a) White Bread v. Brown Bread

The outer protective coats of the wheat grain, that is the *bran*, cannot be digested. In milling, this fraction of the grain is removed, and even so-called "wholemeal" flour rarely comprises more than 92% of the total grain. The process of milling consists of a series of operations in which the grain is broken up and the different structures of which it is composed separated more or less completely from each other. By proper control of the process it is possible to produce a fine *patent flour* comprising about 60% of the original grain which consists almost entirely of starch and from which the major proportion of the protein, fat, mineral matter and vitamins have been removed. A flour thus representing 60% of the wheat from which it is made is described as being of 60% *extraction*, or of 60% *extraction rate*. It is possible for the millers to produce a flour of any *extraction rate* they choose, from a "wholemeal" brown flour of 92%, to a wartime "National" flour of 85%, or to an everyday white flour of 70% extraction, or a fine patent quality for pastry at 60% extraction rate.

The effect on the nutritive value of the flour, and of bread made from it, of gradually *reducing* the extraction rate, and thereby simultaneously increasing the whiteness, is as follows:

(i) *Advantages*

1. The whiter flours contain less fat and are therefore less susceptible to rancidity and off-flavour on storage.
2. The whiter flours possess technical advantages in baking, that is, they produce loaves which are generally accepted as being of superior quality.
3. They contain less *phytic acid* (see Chapter 7) to hamper the absorption of calcium from the diet.

(ii) *Disadvantages*

1. White flour contains less *vitamin B₁, riboflavin, niacin, protein, iron*.

In Great Britain, all flour used for breadmaking has added to it the following substances:

Calcium carbonate (chalk) 14 oz. per 280-lb. sack to increase the calcium content by about 30 mg. per oz.

Vitamin B₁ (added as pure thiamine) to give a total content of 0·07 mg. per oz.

Niacin (added as the pure substance) to give a total content of 0·45 mg. per oz.

Iron to give a total content of 0·46 mg. per oz.

White bread is an attractive and digestible food and can, even when not enriched, form part of a satisfactory *mixed diet*. On the other hand, a poor or ignorant person attempting to live on a diet made up predominantly of white bread, margarine, jam and tea would eventually suffer from a deficiency of B-vitamins (as well as from vitamin C deficiency due to lack of fruit or vegetables). It is to prevent even the possibility of this occurring that vitamin B₁ and niacin are added in Great Britain as well as calcium carbonate and iron.

(b) Rice

The same nutritional considerations apply to rice as to wheat. The more thoroughly the grain is milled and the outer coats removed, the smaller are the proportions of vitamin B_1 that remain. This is of much more practical significance in the diets of the millions of people for whom rice is a staple because it often constitutes a far larger proportion of the total diet than wheat does in bread-eating countries. Yet, although an outbreak of beri-beri due to vitamin-B_1 deficiency is always a danger for poor people in the East, it is difficult to persuade them to eat anything less than white rice (as we do) because they find the darker grades less attractive. In certain districts, however, it is the custom to parboil the rice before milling. This drives vitamin B_1 from the outer coats into the grain where it subsequently remains in the milled materials. Efforts have been made to have this process more widely adopted.

The vitamin-B_1 content of different grades of rice is as follows:

	Vitamin B_1 (mg. per oz.)	
	Direct milling	*After parboiling*
Husked only	0·11	0·07
Polished once	0·04	0·07
Polished twice	0·03	0·06
Polished three times (as eaten in U.K.)	0·02	0·05

2. Dairy Produce

Milk.

Milk is a remarkably valuable food which combines the following qualities:

(i) It is a good source of a complete and readily digestible protein; this protein forms the main component of cheese.

   (ii) It is the main dietary source of *calcium* and also contains vitamin D which contributes to the absorption of the calcium, and vitamin A.

   (iii) It is a major source of B-vitamins.

   (iv) The fatty portion, that is the cream, contributes vitamin A to the diet, and vitamin D.

Milk is *not* a complete food and cannot safely constitute the sole component of the diet. It is deficient in *iron* and the small amount of *vitamin C* in it may easily be lost through the action of light or through heating.

The Pasteurisation of Milk

The high nutritive value of milk and the fact that it is a liquid makes it very susceptible to infection by micro-organisms. There are naturally occurring in the atmosphere and in the general environment numerous organisms which, while not producing any symptoms of illness, cause changes to occur in the composition of milk as they gain entry and proliferate in it. These are the causes of souring and of the deterioration observed when the milk "turns". Besides these, however, there are other bacteria that grow readily in milk and cause disease when the milk is subsequently drunk. These organisms may be derived from the following sources:

1. From infected cows.
2. From human carriers who handle milk.
3. From utensils and dairy equipment.
4. *Clean milk may be infected by being mixed with contaminated milk.*

This is an ever-present hazard when large quantities of milk are bulked together to provide supplies for schools and other numerous communities of people. In order to destroy bacterial infection in milk, it is subjected to the *process of pasteurisation*. Pasteurisation is usually done by heating it to 162°F. for 15 seconds. This process is sufficient to destroy the tuberculosis bacillus, which is the most resistant of the more likely infective organisms.

Pasteurisation has no effect on the important nutrients in milk. It causes a small loss of vitamin B_1 and a reduction in vitamin C. It is for this reason that alternative sources of vitamin C, for example, orange juice, should be given to artificially fed infants whose diet is mainly composed of pasteurised cow's milk. These losses in nutrients are more than counterbalanced by safety from infection.

Milk Products

  (i) *Cheese* is composed of the protein and fat from milk. It is also an excellent source of calcium. Different types of cheeses contain differing proportions of fat and moisture.

  (ii) *Butter* is composed mainly of the fat fraction of milk. It contains vitamin A and vitamin D in amounts that vary with the breed of cow and season of the year. In summer when the cows have grass to eat in the sunshine the vitamin content of butter made from their milk is twice as high as when they are fed indoors on hay.

(iii) *Dried milk*

  (*a*) *Dried whole milk* contains all the milk nutrients (except vitamin C). Only the water is removed. It is the main constituent of infant foods.

  (*b*) *Dried skimmed milk* is a valuable source of protein, calcium and B-vitamins but the butter fat has been removed and it consequently contains no vitamin A or vitamin D. *It must not, therefore, be used unsupplemented as an infant food.*

  (*c*) *Evaporated milk*, like dried whole milk, contains all the milk nutrients. Part of the original water only has been removed. *Condensed milk* is a similar product but has sugar added to it.

3. Meat

(i) *Lean meat*, whether mutton or beef, is made up of the muscle fibres of the animal. Its components are:

(*a*) *Protein.*

(*b*) *Mineral salts*, including particularly *iron*.

(*c*) *B-vitamins* of which *niacin* and *vitamin B_{12}* are nutritionally significant.

(*d*) Water.

(*e*) *Extractives.* These are not themselves of much nutritional value but they give meat its flavour and stimulate the flow of digestive juices.

Apart from its nutritional value particularly as a source of animal protein, meat is important as forming *the centre of a meal* in which other foodstuffs, including fresh vegetables, are consumed. It is for this reason, rather than for any superiority in nutrient content, that "prime" meat is more highly prized than cheaper cuts.

(ii) *Fat.* The fat in meat, whether it occurs as obvious fatty portions or as "marbling", is nutritionally significant primarily—as other fats are—as a source of calories.

(iii) *Bacon and pork.* Pig meat often contains more fat than other meats. Its vitamin B_1 content is also higher.

(iv) *Liver and kidney.* These meats contain less fat than muscle meats. Liver is *very rich in vitamin A.*

4. Fish

Fish, like meat, is a valuable source of *animal protein*. It is also a useful source of *calcium*, particularly when the bones are eaten as with sardines, whitebait and often with canned salmon. Marine fish are a source of *iodine*. Nutritionally fish can be divided into two classes:

138

(i) *Fat fish* (containing 5–20% of fat). These include herring, mackerel, salmon, eel, etc. The fat from fish is a source of vitamins A and D.

(ii) *White fish* (containing about 2% of fat). These include cod, haddock, sole, whiting, etc.

5. Vegetables

(i) *Green vegetables.* These are the principal source of *vitamin C* in the diet. They also supply *vitamin A-active carotene.* The percentage of water in green vegetables is large and they are therefore, weight for weight, a poor source of calories, protein and fat.

(ii) *Root vegetables. Potatoes,* although they are about 75% water, contribute a significant number of *calories* and a useful amount of protein to the diet. When they are eaten regularly each day they provide a valuable supply of *vitamin C.*

Carrots, as was described in Chapter 9, are a major source of *vitamin A-active carotene.* Sweet potatoes also contain vitamin A-activity.

Turnips and swedes are more than 90% water. They provide few calories but contribute some *vitamin C.*

(iii) *Peas and beans. Fresh or frozen green peas* are similar in nutritional value to green vegetables. They contain *vitamin C* and *vitamin A-activity. Canned green peas* possess similar nutritional characteristics. "*Processed peas*", however, do *not* supply vitamins A and C; they are made by canning soaked and coloured dried peas.

Dried peas and beans contain no vitamin C and negligible vitamin A-activity. They ought not, therefore, to be considered dietetically as "vegetables" at all. They contribute *protein* to the diet.

6. Fruit

(i) *Fresh fruit* are primarily a source of *vitamin C*. Blackcurrants, citrus fruits such as oranges, grapefruit and lemons and some seasonal varieties including strawberries and gooseberries are rich sources. Apples are not particularly rich in vitamin C but nevertheless make a useful contribution to a diet not otherwise providing much fresh food. In general *canned* and *frozen* fruits provide about as much vitamin C as fresh fruits. Properly prepared *fruit juices* may be good sources of vitamin C but it is always prudent to verify that this is so. *Commercial fruit drinks*, lemonade, orangeade and the like are usually marketed for their palatability rather than their nutritive value and do not contain any vitamin C at all.

(ii) *Dried fruit*, currants, raisins, dates, figs, etc., contain *sugar* and hence provide calories. They do not contain vitamin C. Prunes and dried apricots contain some *vitamin A-activity*.

(iii) *Nuts* are rich in *protein* and *fat* and consequently are a rich source of *calories*. They contain quite large concentrations of *vitamin B$_1$*.

CHAPTER SIXTEEN

COOKING

COOKING involves the application of heat to foodstuffs. When the heat is directly applied the operation becomes *baking, roasting* or *grilling*. If the heat is applied through the intermediacy of water or steam the operation is *boiling* (or simmering) or *steaming*. Finally, the heat may be applied at a higher temperature by means of hot oil or fat: this is *frying*. Cooking has three effects:

(a) *It improves the palatability of the food*. This may have a very direct effect on nutrition because, as has been said before, no matter how nutritious a diet may be it cannot exert its effect if it is not eaten.

(b) *It improves the digestibility of foods*. Apart from the favourable effect on digestion and absorption derived from the flow of digestive juices engendered by the sight and smell of a well-cooked meal, heat breaks up the starch granules of cereal foods such as raw flour and potato and renders them more digestible. It also breaks down the fibres of connective tissue in meat and renders it also more digestible and tender.

(c) *It destroys many of the harmful organisms* with which the food may have become contaminated.

THE EFFECT OF COOKING ON THE DIFFERENT NUTRIENTS

1. Carbohydrate

(i) *Starch*. Starch, which as was described in Chapter 2, is the form in which carbohydrate is stored in cereal grains and, in tubers such as the potato, is held in the plant in the form of granules. These granules are quite resistant to digestion if flour or potato is eaten raw. The effect of heat and moisture in boiling potatoes or baking bread or cakes is to cause the starch grains to absorb water, to swell and finally to rupture the granules. The starch that is released is gelatinised, in which form it can readily be digested. This effect of cooking is shown diagrammatically in Figure 12.

Cells and starch grains
of uncooked potato

Cooked potato showing the
starch gelatinised and many
of the cells ruptured

FIGURE 12.

The effect of boiling on the starch grains in a potato.

If cooked starch is heated further, as occurs when bread is made into toast or when pie-crust is browned in the oven, the large chemical molecule of starch, which is a long and complex chain, becomes broken into fragments. These fragments are called *dextrins*. If carbohydrate is subjected to further undue heat, its chemical structure is completely disrupted and part will appear as black elemental carbon. This charcoal cannot be absorbed and is of no nutritional value.

2. Protein

Proteins, though all belonging to the same class of compounds, namely those composed of combined units of *amino acids*, may belong to one of several groups.

(i) *Soluble proteins* occur in milk, in blood plasma and in egg white. When certain of these are heated, their chemical structure is changed and they become *denatured*. This may cause the protein to *coagulate*. The most obvious example of this reaction occurs when an egg is hard boiled and the albumin of the white changes from a soluble substance into a firm insoluble solid.

(ii) *Muscle protein*, which is the lean portion of meat, is composed of elastic fibres. Cooking *denatures* the protein of these fibres and causes them to shrink. This is the reason for the pronounced reduction in the size of a steak while it is being cooked. Cooking does not directly increase the digestibility of meat *protein*. It does improve the digestibility of *meat* as such, however, by breaking down the tough fibres of connective tissue surrounding the muscle fibres and thus making the protein itself more readily accessible to the digestive enzymes. This effect is apparent in the tenderness of properly cooked meat. The same effect can be obtained by pounding a steak with a piece of wood. The elastic tissues in tendons and sinews—that is to say, gristle—are not affected by cooking and are virtually indigestible.

Fish protein like meat protein is digestible uncooked and raw fish is indeed eaten in a number of communities in different parts of the world. This is a dangerous practice and may lead to food poisoning or infection by harmful parasites. Fish, again like meat, is rendered less tough after it is cooked because the heat ruptures the connective tissues which in life maintain the integrity of the muscular structure. A further and more direct effect of cooking on the nutritional value of fish is that the heat gets rid of an enzyme present in raw fish which destroys vitamin B_1.

3. Fat

(i) The heat used in most normal cooking has little effect on the chemical composition of fat or on its nutritional value.

(ii) If fat is subjected to prolonged heating, when it is exposed to air it may become oxidised and develop rancid flavours. This occurs when pastry, for example, in which fat is dispersed over a very large surface of cooked flour, is re-heated or kept hot in the oven. The presence of oxidised fat in the diet may have a harmful effect by destroying vitamin E.

(iii) When fat is seriously overheated in cooking its chemical structure may be disrupted. Fat is, as was described in Chapter 3, a chemical combination of fatty acids, three of which are linked to a single unit of glycerol (glycerine). Strong heating breaks these linkages and may convert the glycerol into *acrolein* which acts as a "tear gas" and has a sharp and painful effect on the eyes.

4. Mineral substances

Cooking *may cause losses* of minerals from the diet because soluble salts are leached out of foods when they are cooked in large volumes of water which are subsequently discarded. On the other hand useful amounts of mineral elements *may be added* to the diet from the water in which the foods are cooked.

(i) *Calcium*. Heat as applied in cooking, causes a slight reduction in the availability of the calcium in *milk*. This effect, however, is not of very great significance. On the other hand, quite substantial supplements of calcium may be obtained from "hard" cooking water. It has been found that when *green vegetables* are cooked in "hard" water the amount of calcium derived from the water may be enough to double their initial content of calcium.

(ii) *Iron.* Cooking may render iron in such foods as meat and wholemeal cereals somewhat more readily available. On the other hand, there is a loss of iron if red juices are allowed to escape from meat and are discarded. Probably the most significant effect of cooking on the effective iron content of the diet is due to the increased amounts derived from *water* and more especially from *iron cooking-vessels and utensils.* This source of iron may be particularly important in underdeveloped countries where a poor diet is eaten but iron cooking-pots are common. On the other hand, if an excess of iron enters food from utensils, *siderosis*, may occur as was described on p. 77.

5. Vitamins

(i) *Fat-soluble vitamins.* Vitamin D is resistant to normal cooking. It is resistant to heat and it is not soluble in water and consequently is not lost in cooking water. *Vitamin A* is also insoluble in water and is not destroyed by heat. It is, however, destroyed if it is exposed to air when spread as a thin layer over a very large surface area. Destruction is particularly rapid when the food is heated. Vitamin A is therefore lost when butter and eggs are mixed into a cake, when it is subjected to heat while dispersed over the large surface provided by the crumb.

(ii) *Water-soluble vitamins*

Vitamin B_1 *(a)* This vitamin is gradually destroyed by the heat of cooking. When especially

145

high temperatures are used, as in baking biscuits, loss of vitamin B_1 may be almost complete.

(*b*) It is readily destroyed by *alkalis*. Consequently, serious losses may occur when baking soda is used in cooking.

(*c*) Vitamin B_1 is soluble in water and losses consequently occur when foods are boiled and the cooking water discarded.

Riboflavin and niacin. These vitamins are more resistant to heat than vitamin B_1 and comparatively small losses occur in cooking due to the temperatures used. Since they are also soluble in water, losses may arise if excessive quantities of cooking water are used and then poured away.

Vitamin C. Improper methods of cooking may seriously deplete the diet of vitamin C

(*a*) Vitamin C is susceptible to *heat*. Cases of scurvy have occurred when too-careful mothers have misguidedly boiled the *milk* given to their babies.

(*b*) *Heat in the presence of air* is particularly destructive of vitamin C. For this reason keeping vegetables hot causes serious losses.

(*c*) *Vitamin C is very soluble in water*. Losses consequently occur when cooking liquors are discarded.

(*d*) Vitamin C is quickly destroyed by *plant enzymes*. These enzymes are themselves destroyed by heat. It is therefore important to bring green vegetables to the boil as quickly as possible to destroy the enzyme that is released from the cells before it can destroy the vitamin C.

(e) Vitamin C is destroyed by traces of *copper*.

THE EFFECT OF COOKING ON THE NUTRITIVE VALUE OF INDIVIDUAL FOODS

The main purpose of cooking is to make food *more palatable*. The principal nutritional effects of the cooking process are, therefore:

1. An increase in food consumption. That is to say, people eat *more* and, as a general rule, digest and absorb more when food is cooked than when it is eaten raw.

2. The nutritional value of one article of food may be *enhanced* by being mixed with other foods. For example, flour contributes mainly carbohydrate to the diet in the form of starch. It also contains some vegetable protein. The addition to it of egg, in making a cake, besides enabling both to be eaten together, improves the nutritional value of the total protein because the amino acids of the egg protein supplement those of the flour protein.

3. The *losses* in nutritional value from cooking already described for the individual nutrients, are far outweighed by the advantages.

Cereals. Cooking (1) bursts the *starch* granules and makes them more digestible. (2) In bread and buns fermented by yeast, the fermentation stretches the elastic strands of the flour *protein* (gluten) and gives an open-grained, palatable article. Little loss of *vitamin* B_1 occurs. At higher temperatures, for example, when biscuits are baked, loss of vitamin B_1 may be substantial.

Meat. Cooking makes meat more acceptable although the digestibility and nutritional value of raw meat may be as good as when it is cooked. The breakdown of connective fibres during cooking makes cooked meat tender and easier to eat and digest. No significant loss of *niacin* or other *B-vitamins* occurs.

Fish, like meat, is rendered more friable by cooking. Cooking destroys an enzyme present in raw fish that otherwise causes destruction of vitamin B_1.

Vegetables. Cooking softens the tough fibres of vegetables; it bursts the starch granules in potatoes and breaks down the rigid structure of dried peas and beans. The most significant effect of cooking on fresh vegetables is the degree of loss of vitamin C. *In potatoes* about half the original vitamin C is lost during the boiling of peeled potatoes partly from the heat and partly in the cooking water. When they are boiled in their skins or fried, the loss is about 25%. Potatoes baked in their skins lose about 15% of their vitamin C. Mashing boiled potatoes causes significant additional loss when the mashing is very thorough. *Green vegetables* boiled by being put into water already boiling lose about half their original vitamin C; if they are put into the water when it is cold and it is subsequently raised to boiling, the loss is much greater.

Note. In considering these losses it is always important to bear in mind (*a*) whether the total diet will contain enough vitamin C even when quite large losses occur and (*b*) whether the use of, say, raw cabbage in salad in place of cooked or potato boiled in its skin in place of the more normal boiled peeled potato will really lead to increased consumption of vitamin C or whether the change in treatment may not lead to a reduction in the amount of cabbage or potato eaten.

COOKING AND THE
AVOIDANCE OF FOOD INFECTIONS

The heat used in cooking can serve as a valuable protection against harmful organisms present in the uncooked food, or in the water used for cooking, or reaching the food from the dirty hands or the nose and throat of people handling it. On the other hand, cooked foods that are themselves allowed to stand about under unsatisfactory conditions may form a dangerous focus for infection. The following are the main kinds of infection likely to be encountered:

(i) *Salmonella* "*food poisoning*". This is due to micro-organisms that are derived from the following sources:

    (*a*) Faeces and urine on the hands of people infected with the micro-organisms who touch food without washing their hands after visiting the lavatory.

    (*b*) The droppings of infected rats and mice that contaminate food in dirty kitchens.

    (*c*) Eggs, particularly ducks' eggs, may carry the infection. It has also been found in dried egg.

    (*d*) Oysters from beds contaminated with sewage. Fish may also be infected.

The foods which are the most common source of *Salmonella* infections are meat pies and other made-up meat dishes. If such items are allowed to stand about in a warm place any infection in them may increase to a dangerous degree.

Infection in raw food is rendered harmless by cooking.

(ii) *Staphylococcal infection*. Food, particularly meat, coughed on or handled by people with fingers affected with boils or whitlows may be infected with "food-poisoning" organisms that produce toxins that cannot be destroyed by cooking.

(iii) *Trichinella in raw pork*. This is a minute worm with which the live pig may have been infected. The heat of cooking makes the meat safe. Raw pork or uncooked sausage containing pork should never be eaten.

CHAPTER SEVENTEEN

MEALS

ADEQUATE nutrition depends on the consumption of the requisite number of calories and the appropriate amounts of protein, calcium, iron, vitamins and other nutrients as set out in Table 14 for different types of people doing varying amounts of work. But although this is certainly so, *people do not ingest nutrients, they eat meals*. In order, therefore, to assess the value of any particular diet and to be able to design a diet to fit any special circumstance, it is necessary to be able to calculate the nutrient content of each of the meals of which a day's diet is composed.

To do this, it is first necessary to understand in nutritional terms what a meal is. It may be quite misleading to think that meals are merely those which we call "breakfast", "dinner" and "tea" and to believe that most people eat only three meals a day. It is equally misleading to imagine that only when hot, cooked food is eaten does one consume a meal. Every item of food and drink consumed during the day (excluding only water) contributes to the total dietary intake and must be taken into consideration when assessing the adequacy or otherwise of specific named meals.

WHAT SHOULD BE THE COMPOSITION OF A MEAL?

The science of nutrition, as we have seen, can provide precise information about the amount of fuel (calories) required for a day's activity and about the amounts of vitamins and other nutrients needed to maintain the human body as an efficient machine. This information, however, is applicable to the requirements for 24 hours rather than for the design of a single meal.

A meal must possess certain qualities to fit it for the environment in which it is to be eaten; but the consideration of greatest importance in practice is: does it fit into the pattern of the total day's diet and at the same time contribute nutrients in the right amount so that, within the whole day the person eating it obtains his or her complete nutritional needs? The desirable composition of any one meal, therefore, is affected by the nature of the other meals eaten in the same day.

Let us consider the dietary pattern of a man working, for example, in a shipyard. His day's food supply might be made up like this:

Meal 1. Breakfast

	Weight of each item	Calories	Protein	Vitamin A	Vitamin C
	oz.		g.	i.u.	mg.
Bread	4½	320	11	0	0
Margarine	⅖	87	0	230	0
Tea*	10	50	1	40	0
		457	12	270	0

Meal 2. "Piece" eaten during the morning

Roll	2	142	5	0	0
Butter	½	42	0	230	0
Cheese	½	58	3	180	0
		242	8	410	0

	Weight of each item	Calories	Protein	Vitamin A	Vitamin C
Meal 3. *Canteen dinner*	oz.		g.	i.u.	mg.
Roast beef	3½	311	15	50	0
Boiled potato	5	105	3	0	10
Boiled cabbage	3	21	1	250	25
Yorkshire pudding	3	186	6	0	0
Steamed jam roll	4	246	4	0	0
Custard	2	66	2	40	0
Tea	9	45	1	40	0
		982	32	380	35

Meal 4. *"Piece" eaten during the afternoon*					
Bread	1¼	89	3	0	0
Jam	½	35	0	0	1
Tea	9	45	1	40	0
		169	4	40	1

Meal 5. *Tea*					
Kipper	6	362	32	300	0
Bread	3	213	7	0	0
Butter	½	105	0	570	0
Tea	18	90	2	80	0
		770	41	950	0

Meal 6. *Supper*					
Beer*	60	600	6	0	0
Biscuits	1	107	3	0	0
Tea	9	45	1	40	0
		752	10	40	0
Total day's consumption		3372	107	2090	36

* For the sake of uniformity tea and beer, although customarily measured in pints, are expressed like the other foods in oz. There are 20 oz. in 1 pint.

These meals and the diet of which they are the parts have been calculated in terms of calories, protein, vitamin A and vitamin C by using the figures given in the Appendix for the composition of different types of food. If required, the calcium, iron or B-vitamin content could also be worked out. In considering whether Meal No. 3, that is, the canteen dinner, is nutritionally satisfactory or not, two steps must be taken:

1. **Is the Total Diet Nutritionally Adequate?** (Yes, it is. It provides enough to eat, i.e. adequate calories for a man doing medium to heavy work and it appears to supply more than the required 20 mg. of vitamin C. One cannot be sure on this point without inspecting the cooking and the methods of serving to make sure that, for example, an exceptionally large amount of vitamin C was not destroyed by keeping the cabbage or potatoes hot for long periods of time before serving them.)

2. **Does the Meal Complement the Nutrients Provided by the Other Meals of the Day?** (Again the answer is yes. But it is important to note that it provides almost *all* the day's requirement of vitamin C. Consequently, the vegetables are essential components of the canteen dinner. It would clearly be wrong to exchange the cabbage for baked beans (which do not contain vitamin C) although tomato would make an acceptable exchange. On the other hand, if it was impossible to provide green vegetables for dinner, no harm would be done if one or other of the mid-shift "pieces" were changed so as to include an orange.)

HOW TO CALCULATE THE COMPOSITION OF A MADE DISH

The composition of the various foods listed in the Appendix has been determined by analysis. It is obviously impossible, however, for the Appendix to include every kind of cooked dish and it is, therefore, necessary for a student of nutrition to be able to assess the nutritional value of made dishes by calculation. In fact, the process is a simple matter of arithmetic although it is always necessary at the same time to consider whether or not there may be some measure of destruction or loss of vitamins or other nutrients due to the method of cooking employed. As a general rule, however, calculations can be carried out as follows.

A recipe lists these ingredients to make 10 lb. of cake:

Flour	5 lb.	Dried egg	5 oz.
Margarine	2 lb.	Baking powder	2 oz.
Sugar	2 lb.	Water	2 pints

The composition of each of these separate items is given in the table of food analysis in the Appendix. The procedure is, therefore, to multiply the composition *per oz.* by *the number of ozs.* used in the recipe; add up the total and divide by 160 (the weight of the finished cake in ozs.). This is shown in the first table on page 155.

ARE HOT MEALS "BETTER" THAN COLD MEALS?

It is often assumed that a hot breakfast is essential to good nutrition or that a hot dinner is *necessarily* better than sandwiches. Although it may happen that hot meals contain a good combination of nutrients well designed to fit into the pattern of the total day's intake, and although a well-cooked hot meal may well be attractive and appealing to the palate, it is by no means axiomatic that a hot meal is always better than a cold one. A nutritionist must always study each on its merits. Consider the following two meals.

1. *A cold snack.* This comprises a cheese roll, a cup of tea and an orange.

2. *A hot dinner.* This meal is made up of roast mutton, cabbage and potato followed by apples and custard.

The nutritional composition of these contrasting meals is shown in the second table on page 155.

	Weight oz.	Calories	Protein g.	Fat g.	Calcium mg.	Iron mg.	Vitamin A i.u.	Vitamin B1 mg.	Ribo-flavin mg.	Niacin mg.	Vitamin C mg.	Vitamin D i.u.
Flour	80	7760	262	72	2000	56	0	5·8	3·2	32	0	0
Margarine	32	6980	0	774	30	3	14400	6·0	0	0	0	1790
Sugar	32	3460	0	0	0	0	0	0	0	0	0	0
Dried egg	5	810	65	59	310	15	4250	0·6	1·8	1	0	340
Baking powder	2	0	0	0	0	0	0	0	0	0	0	0
	160	19,010	327	865	2340	74	18,650	5·4	5·0	33	0	2130
Composition per oz.		119	2·0	5·4	15	0·5	116	0·03*	0·30	·20	0	13

* 25% has been deducted as loss of vitamin B1 due to the pressure of baking powder during cooking.

	Weight oz.	Calories	Protein g.	Fat g.	Calcium mg.	Iron mg.	Vitamin A i.u.	Vitamin B1 mg.	Ribo-flavin mg.	Niacin mg.	Vitamin C mg.
1. The snack											
Roll	3·5	252	5·4	1·4	56	1·7	0	0·19	0·10	1·0	0
Butter	0·3	63	0·3	7·0	1	0	342	0	0	0	0
Cheese	2·0	234	14·2	19·6	460	0·4	740	0·02	0·28	0·2	0
Tea	10·0	50	1·0	1·0	30	0	40	0	0·10	0·2	0
Orange	2·0	20	0·4	0	24	0·2	56	0·04	0·02	0·2	32
Total		619	24·3	29·0	570	2·3	1178	0·25	0·50	1·4	32
2. The hot meal											
Mutton	2·4	225	9·0	21·0	6	1·5	33	0·12	0·12	3·0	0
Cabbage	3·0	21	1·2	0	54	0·9	255	0·06	0·06	0·3	24
Potato	4·0	84	2·4	0	8	0·8	12	0·13	0·08	1·2	4
Apples	3·0	36	0·3	0	3	0·3	12	0·04	0	0·3	2
Custard	2·0	66	1·8	2·2	70	0	40	0·01	0·04	0	0
Total		402	14·7	23·2	141	3·5	340	0·36	0·30	4·8	30*

* 60% deducted from the cabbage and 50% from the potato as cooking losses.

For these two particular meals (the same conclusions might not hold for others, of course), the cold snack provided more calories, protein, calcium, vitamin A, riboflavin and vitamin C than the hot meal. An important reason for this was that the cold meal, by including the orange, contained vitamin C which is commonly lacking in snacks of this sort.

HOW MANY MEALS A DAY?

The best number of meals a day to suit different people living different types of lives is very much more a matter of liking and custom rather than one of nutritional requirement. There are, however, a number of guiding principles that can usefully be followed:

(*a*) 4 or 5 hours after a meal there is a tendency for the level of glucose circulating in the bloodstream to fall. This is why people sometimes feel faintness and exhaustion (or bad temper) if they are called upon to do physical work before breakfast or if the period between meals is much prolonged. It is generally considered to be good nutritional practice to have fairly frequent meals throughout the working day.

(*b*) Children, whose energy demands are high but the capacity of whose stomachs is limited, benefit particularly from food every 3–4 hours. The urge felt by children to eat sweets and apples "between meals" is partly a reflection of their nutritional demands for readily available calories.

(*c*) Every item eaten "between meals" is part of the day's total nutritional intake. Indeed, the decision of when food is a "meal" or is something eaten "between meals" is from the nutritional point of view quite an arbitrary one. It is important, therefore, for a nutritionist assessing the adequacy of the diet of a man, a woman or a child to take into account the composition of alcoholic drinks and salted peanuts, or of coffee and biscuits, or of sweets and ice-cream consumed as casual items.

WASTE

The nutritional composition of the diet derived from the different meals of the day can only be calculated from the amounts of *food actually eaten*. If a nutritionist is set the task of planning the meals for, say, a hostel for schoolchildren, or for factory workers, or any other category of people, it is essential that the amount of raw food obtained makes allowances for the losses from waste that always occur at each of the following stages:

(a) *waste at the "wholesale" level*. There will be a proportion of waste in sacks of potatoes, sides of bacon and whole cheeses.

(b) *"as purchased" waste*. This is shown in the figures given in the Appendix. They represent potato peelings, cheese rind, meat bones and the like.

(c) *cooking waste*. Careful weighing will show that significant amounts are lost as residues in saucepans and cooking-pots. These losses vary depending on the scale of the cooking operation. The *percentage* loss in scrambling one egg will be greater than in preparing scrambled egg for twenty people.

(d) *plate waste*. In polite society and when ample supplies are available, account must be taken of the waste of meat fat, fish, crumbs, etc., left as waste on people's plates.

Note. An average figure sometimes used to account for cooking waste and plate waste taken together is 10%.

CHAPTER EIGHTEEN

DIETS

THE combination of meals which people eat constitutes their diet. Although as a matter of convenience it is usual to consider the composition of the different meals *eaten in a single day* and to calculate whether the total nutrient content of these meals provides the requirements for health which were discussed in Chapter 14, it is quite common to find that there are rhythms in diet which recur at different intervals. For example the nutritional composition of the Sunday diet is usually quite different from that eaten on week-days. As we have already seen, one of the commonest deficiencies in the nutritional value of the diet in industrial communities is a shortage of fresh vegetables. This leads to an inadequate consumption of vitamin C. It is, however, possible for a man whose diet during the week, made up from sandwiches midday and a high tea at night, contains only marginal amounts of vitamin C to obtain his needs for vitamin C from the "2 veg." that are served with his joint on Sundays. It should be added that this is dangerous nutritional practice. Should he be late for his dinner two Sundays running and the vitamin C be lost by the vegetables having been kept hot in the oven, he may expect his health to begin to suffer.

As we have seen in the earlier chapters of his book, *the proper design for an adequate diet is a variety and amount of different foods sufficient to provide each day the requirements of nutrients set out in Table* 14. There are a number of principles that can be used as a guide to the achievement of this object.

DIETS FOR YOUNG CHILDREN

Their mother's milk is a satisfactory diet for infants during their first few months of life *provided that they can obtain enough of it*. Cow's milk, either liquid or (as is more usual) dried, can be modified by the addition of sugar and water to provide the approximate amounts of calories, protein, carbohydrate and fat. Cow's milk, however, is nutritionally defective in a number of respects:

(i) it is low in vitamin C and such vitamin C as it does contain is readily lost during the processing of the milk. Infants, therefore, require an early supplementary source of vitamin C in the form of orange juice, rose-hip syrup, etc.

(ii) it is particularly lacking in iron; consequently it is good practice to begin to add gravy, sieved vegetables, egg yolk and chopped meat at quite an early age before the infant's supplies of stored iron become exhausted.

(iii) in Northern climates, a supplementary supply of vitamin D is required.

DIETS FOR CHILDREN OF SCHOOL AGE

It will be found that the problems of designing diets for children to contain the nutrients set out in Table 14 arise from two principal causes:

(i) children's requirements are comparatively high while the capacity of their stomachs is limited. It is, therefore, sensible to see that they are given *a sufficient number of meals*.

(ii) it must also be recognised that children may develop likes and dislikes which, while they need not be given unreasonable attention, must be taken into account when they arise. This can best be done by providing sufficient variety to enable a child who may have a distaste for, let us say, milk to obtain protein and calories by eating more cheese or even good quality ice-cream.

DIETS FOR ADOLESCENTS

As will have been seen from earlier chapters and from Table 14, adolescents possess nutritional needs that exceed in many respects almost all other categories. These increased requirements occur just at a time when the young people may be launching out on their own and when their attention is devoted to their jobs, their clothes and their love affairs rather than their diet. It is for this reason particularly important for nutritionists to give special thought to this group.

FEEDING ATHLETES

Athletes are no exception to the nutritional principles already described in this book. When they undertake long bouts of strenuous training, their requirements for calories are increased, but the nutritional composition of their diet as a whole should be exactly the same as that set out in Table 14 for a heavy worker or a very heavy worker. The nutritional value of a diet for an athlete can, therefore, be taken as being governed by the following rules:

1. *There is no magic formula,* no special consumption of vitamin C or vitamin B_1, no excess ingestion of phosphate or of the protein of beef steak or yoghurt that will give an athlete superior strength or agility.

2. Certain athletic events, for example, marathon running or long-distance swimming or cycling, *demand a very large expenditure of energy for a prolonged period.* Under these circumstances calories (in the form of sugar or glucose, e.g. barley sugar, acid drops, etc.) should be given at fairly frequent intervals. If the strenuous events are undertaken in hot

weather, replacement of water and salt (see Chapter 6) is also important.

3. Success in sport is only partly a matter of physiology and nutritional fitness. Equally or more important are *will-to-win and nerve*. It follows that athletes are often in a state of nervous strain. It is important, therefore, that they should take their meals sufficiently long before they compete (say 2 hours), that they should like what they are given, and that their food should be well cooked and digestible.

DIETS FOR CERTAIN SPECIAL CONDITIONS

1. Dyspepsia

This term covers any pain or discomfort associated with the consumption of food. It may be due to a number of conditions requiring expert medical treatment which obviously cannot be discussed in detail in this book. There are, however, a number of principles by which the nutritionist should be guided in designing diets for people who suffer from dyspepsia:

(a) Although some foods must be avoided and others are better suited for dyspeptics *the diet as a whole must provide the full requirement of nutrients* as set out in Table 14.

(b) Dyspepsia may be caused by *lack of teeth* or by badly fitting dentures. If this is so, appropriate "nutritional" treatment is to see that the sufferer is fitted with an adequate set of teeth. He can then consume a normal diet.

(c) As was described in Chapter 13, satisfactory digestion is to an important degree dependent on a calm mind and on the absence of *tension and worry*. Another "nutritional" approach is to try to make the dyspeptic happy and relaxed and to give him sufficient time for his meals.

(d) *Items to avoid* are spirits, strong tea or coffee, pickles and condiments, fibrous foods such as raw vegetables and unripe fruit and fruit with pips and skins (including currants and raisins), and highly seasoned meats or fish. *Items to encourage* are milk, butter and eggs (but not fried eggs); tender meat and chicken; boiled white fish; white bread (but not new) and well-cooked cereals such as rice pudding; and sieved vegetables and fruits.

2. Diabetes

Diabetes is a disease in which the ability of the body to manage sugar is lost to a greater or lesser degree. If a diabetic eats sugar it first piles up in his blood to such a degree that he is in danger of being "poisoned" by it. On the other hand, because his body cannot store excess sugar expeditiously, losses of sugar occur in the urine. Diabetes cannot be cured but it can be treated effectively by injections of *insulin*. But satisfactory treatment with insulin requires that the diabetic sufferer eats every day a uniform diet containing precisely the same amount of carbohydrate.

Since it would be unreasonable to expect a diabetic to eat *the same menu* every day, it is quite essential for people who have diabetes (*a*) to know at least something about nutrition and (*b*) to weigh all the foods they eat. The exact nutritional value of the diet, that is the amount of carbohydrate, protein and fat, must be worked out for each patient by a doctor. It will, of course, depend on the severity of the disease in relation to the physique of the particular individual and the amount of insulin injected each day. This having been done, however, the patient, equipped with his balance for weighing food, will be given exact details of a day's menu with the precise weights of each item. He will also be given a list showing permissible exchanges. For example, if he is allowed 1 oz. of bread for breakfast, he may if he wishes, eat ¾ oz. of toast instead (they both contain about 16 g. of carbohydrate). Or, for that matter, he may abandon the bread for ⅔ oz. of cornflakes (but with *no* sugar). The following are examples of the weights of different foods that may be exchanged to maintain the necessary balance of protein, carbohydrate and fat. It can readily be seen from this how important it is for his own

FIGURE 13.

Accurate balance for weighing foods in carrying out an individual dietary survey.

well-being that the sensible diabetic weighs his food carefully and understands at least something of nutrition.

(i) *Carbohydrate equivalents*

1 oz. bread, ¾ oz. toast, ⅔ oz. cornflakes, 2 oz. cooked rice, ⅔ oz. jam, 10 oz. raspberries, 5 oz. apples, 3 oz. bananas, 2½ oz. boiled potatoes, 1½ oz. chips.

(ii) *Protein equivalents*

1 oz. lean beef or mutton, 1 oz. chicken, 1 egg (2 oz.), 1 oz. cheese, 1½ oz. fish.

(iii) *Fat equivalents*

½ oz. butter or margarine, ½ oz. cooking fat or oil, ¾ oz. salad cream.

3. Allergy

Each individual person in the world possesses his own finger-prints and, in the same way, possesses certain subtle individual peculiarities in the protein that he can tolerate mixed with his own. For this reason, skin grafts can only very rarely be made from one person to another and then mostly only from one identical twin to another. But this intolerance to foreign protein is not absolute. Blood transfusions can be tolerated provided the right *type* of blood is used in each case. When most of us eat foods, their proteins are completely broken down by the process of digestion before they are absorbed (as described in Chapter 13). There are, however, some people who absorb, unchanged, some of the protein from certain foods. This protein is "foreign" to the human body and causes a reaction which, if it is strong, is called an *anaphylactic shock*. This may be severe enough to cause death. Weaker responses—mild nettle-rash, malaise, headaches or prostration—are called *allergic reactions*.

Little is known about the cause of food allergy. It is commonest in infants and young children and may fade away or disappear as people get older. The dietary treatment of food allergy is to find out which food produces the undesirable effect and delete it from the diet, substituting another of equivalent nutritional value. The following items are known to produce an allergic reaction in some individuals:

1. *Wheat*. The serious disease of infants, *coeliac disease*, is now known to be caused by an intolerance to the wheat protein, *gluten*.

2. *Milk*. It has recently been shown that a certain number of infants can become sensitised to cow's milk protein. If these babies then accidentally inhale some of the contents of their stomach while they are asleep—as may easily happen—they may suffer an allergic "anaphylactic" shock and be found afterwards dead in their cots. This new discovery provides at

least one good reason in favour of breast feeding whenever possible for infants during the first few months of their lives.

3. *Eggs.*

4. *Fish and shell-fish.*

5. *Certain types of meat.*

6. *Fruit* (oranges, bananas, tomatoes).

7. *Nuts*, *celery*, *mustard.*

8. *Broad beans.* These are believed to be the cause of a peculiar disease, *favism*, particularly affecting people from Sicily.

ASSESSING THE ADEQUACY OF DIETS

The main part of this book has been concerned with a description of the nutrients that are required for health, with their function in the body, and with the amounts of each which are needed by different categories of people. When a nutritionist has to deal with *groups* of people, the *average requirements* detailed in Table 14 in Chapter 14 can be appropriately used. But *averages* will not always do. For sufferers from certain diseases, of which diabetes is one, certain modifications need to be made in the balance of nutrients; with other conditions, such as dyspepsia or food allergy, selection of special foods to provide the nutrients must be made. And whenever a *single particular individual* is being considered, whether he or she is a diabetic or a healthy person, although the known *average requirements* will form an essential guide, it must always be remembered that *individual study* is necessary in order to judge the individual need of the person in question. It is this fact that makes the practice of medicine, however firmly it may be based on science, an art requiring experience and judgement. Nutrition is a science but when it is applied to the consideration of the well-being of a single individual it too calls for judgement and wisdom.

1. Assessing the Adequacy of a Community Diet

The nutritionist needs to obtain a record of the total food supplies available during any stated period. These will comprise foods available from the market, from local sources such as allotments or gardens, and food drawn from stocks on hand. Appropriate adjustment must be made to allow for wastage and loss at each stage in the chain of distribution. The *average* nutritional value of the food available *per head* of the community can then be calculated. The *average requirement per head* can also be calculated provided the number of children at each age, of heavy workers, sedentary workers, etc., of each sex is known. When the nutrients available per head are compared with the nutrient requirement per head, any deficiency can be readily seen. A further point to be remembered, however, is whether the distribution of nutrients within a community, whose *average* nutrient supply may be sufficient, is in fact uniform—for example, that the poor or the old or the self-sacrificing mother of a family may not be going short.

2. Assessing the Adequacy of a Household Diet

This can be done by recording the total amount of food brought into the household during some convenient period: a week is usually employed. Supplies will comprise (1) the weekly purchases of food, (2) any foods brought in from the garden, fish caught or game shot, (3) food taken from the storeroom during the period of survey, (4) food obtained as meals eaten outside the house, at restaurants, canteens, as school meals or milk and (5) miscellaneous articles including chocolates and sweets, glasses of beer or cups of tea. Before the nutritional value of the total food supply is calculated from the figures given in food tables, it is of course necessary to deduct an allowance for cooking losses and wastage. When the total nutritional value has been calculated it can, as before, be divided by the number of individuals in the household to give the *average nutritional value* of the diet. This can then be compared with the *average nutritional requirement* so that any deficiencies can be detected.

3. Assessing the Adequacy of an Individual Diet

(*a*) *A general picture* of the nutritional composition of a diet can be obtained by taking *a dietary history*, that is to say by interrogating an individual about his or her diet. This is best done by asking the question "what did you have for break-fast yesterday?" and then going systematically meal by meal through the day. By this means a very much more accurate picture can be obtained than by asking such questions as: "Do you eat potatoes?" A somewhat more precise estimate of the quantities of each individual item can be reached if the nutritionist carries with him a series of models so that when the person whose diet is being studied says that he ate a slice of beef, the nutritionist can point to several weighed portions and ask which was nearest in size to the one eaten.

(*b*) *Calculated nutritional value.* This can be obtained by arranging for the individual under study to record every item eaten *and weigh it* on an accurate balance. The nutritional value can then be assessed by calculation from food tables. This method, which involves a considerable amount of work, gives a result, the accuracy of which depends on the appropriateness of the food tables used. It must always be remembered, however, that foods are themselves the products of living things, whether plants or animals, and that they too have their own individuality. Food tables, by their very nature, can only supply *average* values.

(*c*) *For detailed nutritional research* it is necessary not only to weigh accurately every article of food and drink consumed but also to analyse representative samples of each. This is the sort of biochemical study that is the basis of much that has been written in this book.

CHAPTER NINETEEN

LIKES, DISLIKES AND NUTRITION

THERE are two cardinal points to remember in the study of the science of nutrition:

1. Nutritional welfare depends on the intake of the nutrients derived from foods in those amounts known to be required by people of a stated age, sex and activity. This is basic to the whole principle of scientific nutrition: that the laws of physiology hold without exception for all *groups*.

2. The second principle worth remembering by a wise nutritionist is that *individuals* vary. Firstly, they may vary by 10 to 15% either way in their calorie demands and the point at which they will or will not show signs of vitamin deficiency. But more important than this, individuals vary in their likes and dislikes for food, in their allergic reactions towards special food items and, above all, in the importance they attach to food in comparison with their interest in other human aspirations. The emotions which compel a convinced Vegan (an advanced form of vegetarian) to bring himself with open eyes to the verge of breakdown from vitamin-B_{12}-deficiency, or the scruples that will deprive an orthodox Jew of nourishment when only pork is to be had, or the civilised revulsion that makes a man embrace death from starvation rather than violate the bodies of the slain—these emotions, if only in a lesser degree, influence what people eat under more ordinary conditions.

It follows from this second principle that a knowledge of the nutritional composition of foods, such as is given in the

Appendix, combined with an understanding of nutritional requirements as described in Chapter 14, is not sufficient to ensure that a satisfactory diet will be made available. People in ordinary life do not behave like experimental rats in a laboratory. If they do not like their food they will not eat it, and if they eat insufficient for their needs they will not function efficiently and may insidiously develop anaemia or vitamin deficiency or one or other of the conditions due to malnutrition.

"A little of what you fancy does you good" is an aphorism that is always being quoted at the working nutritionist. It is only true if what you "fancy" is indeed what you *need* and if, because you fancy it, you eat it. We are so much creatures of habit that we may easily become used to what does *not* do us good—yet we "fancy" it just the same. Children may quickly learn to "fancy" sugary sweets and by so doing damage their teeth and by satiating their appetites become unable to consume their needs of protein, calcium and vitamins. Obese ladies may "fancy" rich cakes between meals and by yielding to their fancy do themselves no good at all but, on the contrary, shorten their life-spans, aggravate their varicose veins and spoil their appearance.

Yet it behoves a nutritionist to pay attention to the likes and dislikes of the people whose diet is his concern. The following factors must be considered:

(a) *Flavour and aroma.* The flavour and aroma of well-cooked food are among the most attractive things which the nutritionist can call upon to make the diets—whose nutrient content he has assessed—acceptable. As a general rule, however, it is true that the chemical substances that give foods their smell and taste do not themselves possess very much nutritional value either good or bad. In Great Britain we like beef and chicken to smell fresh and venison and pheasant to smell stale—

169

or, as we should put it "high". We also prefer an egg to appear fresh, whether or not it has been in cold-storage for a twelve-month, whereas the Chinese we are told relish "high" eggs as a delicacy. It must be remembered that most of the chemical changes that so markedly alter the flavour and smell of fresh food as it grows older have no significant effect on its nutritional value.

(b) *Colour*. Colour exerts a remarkable effect on what people think about their food and for this reason it may cause them to change their diet either for the better or the worse. In the United States, the dairymen for a long time insisted that there be a law that margarine should not be coloured. Consequently it had to be sold looking like lard. The nutritional value of the white margarine was just as good as butter-coloured margarine but few people would eat it. On the other hand, manufacturers of flour confectionery often add yellow dye to cakes that do not contain egg to give them the appearance that they do. Faced with this situation, the nutritionist must consider whether the lack of the protein, iron and vitamin A that might have been obtained from the egg is or is not counterbalanced by the gain of nutrients obtained by the consumption of a cake which might not have been eaten at all had it been uncoloured. Each situation of this sort needs to be judged on its merits.

The dyes that are used in food manufacture are nowadays restricted to those permitted by the public health authorities. In Great Britain, the Food Standards Committee of the Ministry of Agriculture, Fisheries and Food has the responsibility of recommending the acceptance or refusal of such dyes. Although the risk to health from consuming these chemical compounds is very slight indeed, it would obviously be safest to forbid the use of dyes entirely. But here again, there must be a balance between the slight advantage in safety on the one hand and the lack of enjoyable and appetising colour on the other. Be this as it may, the intelligent nutritionist will bear in mind the importance that the consumer attaches to colour when he or she designs a diet from foods, which combined, are to supply a day's nutritional requirement.

(c) *Texture and keeping quality.* A number of substances have been developed by the chemical industry to improve the technical quality of manufactured foods and to extend the length of time during which they can safely be stored. Among these are the following:

(i) *Flour "improvers".* There are several chemical substances, of which *chlorine dioxide* is one of the more popular, that are used to produce a larger loaf of more even structure than would otherwise be obtainable. In addition, there are other substances that act as *anti-staling agents.* The materials now employed have no known nutritional effect, good or bad.

(ii) *Fat "extenders".* These are substances that produce much the same effect in baking cakes as fat. They therefore enable the manufacturer to produce a palatable article while economising in fat. The nutritional result is to reduce the calorific value of the article and give a lower fat consumption.

(iii) *Chemical preservatives.* In Great Britain only two chemical preservatives may be used in foods. These are benzoic acid and sulphurous acid. Both these substances, used in the small concentrations permitted by the public health authorities, extend the life of foodstuffs by an appreciable degree. Sulphurous acid is destructive of vitamin B_1. In recent years, antibiotics, and particularly aureomycen, have been used as food preservatives. Although antibiotics are mostly destroyed by cooking, the use of these materials for purposes other than the medical treatment of disease is not very advisable for fear that resistant bacteria may gradually develop. A few other substances are permitted in certain special circumstances.

(iv) *Preservation by canning and freezing.* These processes have been of very great nutritional benefit because they have made it possible to preserve perishable foods when they are available and transport them to distant cities for use all the year round. The heat used in *canning* causes some reduction in the content of B-vitamins in such foods as meat and some destruction in vitamin C in vegetables. In general, however, the less rigorous cooking needed to prepare canned foods for the table causes less loss than domestic cooking. In balance, there-fore, the nutritional value of canned food when it is eaten is at least equal to that of the same food fresh after it has been cooked in the normal way.

Freezing is also a useful method for preserving food and for making it possible to provide an attractive and varied diet. The temperature used for commercial freezing is very much lower than that to be found in a domestic refrigerator and frozen foods can therefore be stored for consider-able periods of time without loss of nutritional value provided they are kept in the frozen state. In freezing fruit and vegetables, account has to be taken of the enzyme systems present in plant cells to which reference was made in Chapter 16. These foods are, therefore, scalded before being frozen— this is the so-called "blanching" process. This causes some loss of vitamin C so that, as with canning, the product as finally prepared for the table has lost about the same proportion of its vitamin C (partly by "blanching" and partly in cooking) as the same fresh food loses in the normal cooking process.

(v) *Dehydration*. Foods can be preserved by the removal of water from them under appropriate conditions. Such foods when rehydrated possess approximately the same nutritional value as fresh cooked foods.

THE TWO SIDES OF A GOOD DIET

A reader who has begun to understand the real problems of teaching himself nutrition—which it is the object of this book to help him (or her) to do—will now have appreciated that there are two ways of assessing a good diet. These are:

1. At the heart of the science of nutrition lies the understanding of the nature of the different nutrients of which the diet is composed: protein, carbohydrate, fat and the calories they supply, minerals of various sorts and the series of vitamins. Each of these performs its particular function and a satisfactory diet *must provide the right amount of each* to meet the needs of each different category of individual, whether he be an infant, a child, a man or a woman, hard working or sedentary, a nursing mother or an old man. And within each category there are individual people whose requirements may diverge to some degree from the average for his group. Thus the first part of the science of nutrition requires knowledge of the weights of each food eaten, its composition in terms of nutrients, an estimate of cooking losses and hence from all this an assessment of the total nutrient intake for the day. This then can be compared with a table of estimated requirements and any deficiency measured and made good.

2. The other aspect of the science of nutrition which can never safely be overlooked is that in all normal communities people eat what they like. And it is important to the nutritionist that they should like what they eat. Liking is a complex process made up partly of custom and tradition, partly derived from nutritional need—after all, it is a true saying that hunger is the best sauce—and partly based on what we consider to be "good quality". Quality is *sometimes* related to nutritional values as, for example, when fresh, crisp vegetables rich in vitamin C are selected in preference to "tired" wilted greens from which much of the vitamin C has been lost. But high quality does not *always* imply superior nutritional value. Prime Hereford beef is "good quality"—the best—but as much protein can be obtained for far less money in the form of mince.

We have now introduced the matter of *money* and no sensible book aiming to help its readers to teach themselves nutrition could come to an end without referring to it. A nutritionally adequate diet costs money in every part of the world. Three quarters of the human population are malnourished because they are poor. Even in the fortunate Western countries there are people who live below the "poverty line" and cannot afford to buy enough of the right foods to provide the nutrients they need. There is a lesson for nutritionists to learn when they consider the deficiencies in the diets of these people. It is the last lesson in this book. It is not sufficient to calculate that a family diet is deficient by so many grams of protein and so many international units of vitamin A, that these deficiencies can be made good by the purchase of this much of haricot beans and that much carrot, that the cost of these is four shillings, and consequently that by increasing the family income by four shillings the nutritional problem will be solved. Give a housewife whose income is this much below the "poverty line" the exact amount of money she needs to bring it up and she will not spend it *all* on

174

food. Some of it will go on clothes, some on comforts for the home—and some will be spent on pleasures, say, cigarettes or a visit to a football match.

Proper nutrition is necessary for health, but health is not merely absence of disease, it is total well-being—and this term covers all sorts of human needs. So when you work out the nutritional requirements of the different members of a family, and then calculate what amounts of different foods will provide the proper quantity of all the nutrients required, remember also to translate these foods into attractive meals that the family will be able to afford and which they will *want* to buy. When you are able to do this, you can then claim to have taught yourself nutrition.

APPENDIX

The Nutritive Composition of representative Samples of Various Foods

(composition per oz. of edible portion)

	Waste %	Calories	Protein g.	Fat g.	Carbo-hydrate g.	Calcium mg.	Iron mg.	Vitamin A i.u.	Vitamin B1 mg.	Ribo-flavin mg.	Niacin mg.	Vitamin C mg.	Vitamin D i.u.
1. Cereal foods													
Barley, pearl, uncooked	0	97	2·2	0·5	20·8	3	0·2	0	0·03	0·01	0·7	0	0
Biscuits, water	0	107	3·4	0·9	21·3	23	0·6	0	0·04	0·03	0·3	0	0
Biscuits, "digestive"	0	130	2·7	5·8	16·8	12	0·4	0	0·04	0·03	0·3	0	0
Bread, white (70% extraction)	0	73	2·3	0·2	15·6	30*	0·2	0	0·01	0·01	0·2	0	0
Bread wholemeal (92% extraction)	0	65	3·1	0·6	11·2	7	0·7	0	0·09	0·05	0·6	0	0
Cornflakes	0	106	2·1	0·1	24·3	3	0·8	0	0	0·02	0·3	0	0
Cornflour, custard powder	0	99	0·2	0·1	24·4	11	0·1	0	0·01	0·02	0·3	0	0
Flour, white (70% extraction)	0	98	2·3	0·3	21·6	40**	0·4	0	0·02	0·01	0·3	0	0
Flour, whole-meal (92% extraction)	0	95	4·3	0·9	17·4	10	1·0	0	0·17	0·06	0·8	0	0
Macaroni, spaghetti, uncooked	0	96	3·0	0·6	19·7	7	0·4	0	·02	0·02	0·3	0	0
Oatmeal, uncooked	0	111	3·4	2·5	18·6	16	1·2	0	0·17	0·04	0·3	0	0
Rice, white, uncooked	0	99	1·8	0·3	22·2	1	0·1	0	0·02	0·02	0·3	0	0
Sago, uncooked	0	97	0·1	0·1	24·0	3	0·3	0	0	0	0	0	0
Semolina, uncooked	0	96	3·0	0·5	19·8	5	0·3	0	0·03	0·01	0·3	0	0
Tapioca, uncooked	0	98	0·1	0	24·3	2	0·1	0	0	0	0	0	0

2. *Dairy products*

Butter	0	211	0·1	23·4	0	4	0	1200†	0	0	0	0	17†
Cheese, Cheddar type	5	117	7·1	9·8	0	230	0·2	400	0·01	0·14	0·1	0	10
Eggs	12	45	3·5	3·3	0·3	17	0·8	300	0·04	0·11	0·1	0	17
Milk, fresh	0	17	0·9	1·0	1·2	34	0	30	0·01	0·04	0·1	1	0·3
Milk, evaporated, unsweetened	0	46	2·4	2·6	3·3	83	0·1	100	0·02	0·10	0·1	0·3	1
Milk, condensed, sweetened	0	89	2·3	2·6	14·1	82	0·1	100	0·03	0·10	0·2	0	1
Milk, dried, full cream	0	138	7·3	7·6	10·1	250	0·2	300	0·08	0·33	0·3	0	3
Milk, dried, skimmed	0	97	10·2	0·2	13·6	350	0·3	10	0·11	0·45		0	0
3. *Fats*													
Cooking fat	0	253	0	28·1	0	0	0	0	0	0	0	0	0
Dripping	0	253	0	28·1	0	0	0	30	0	0	0	0	8
Margarine	0	218	0	24·1	0	1	0·1	600††	0	0	0	0	60††
4. *Fish*													
Cod, white fish, uncooked	45	21	4·5	0·3	0	7	0·3	0	0·02	0·04	0·6	0	0
Cod, fried in batter	35	57	5·3	3·4	1·4	24	0·3	0	0·01	0·03	0·4	0	0
Haddock, smoked	45	22	5·1	0·2	0	8	0·3	0	0·02	0·04	0·6	0	0
Herring	30	47	4·5	3·3	0	28	0·4	40	0·08	0·08	1·0	0	250
Kipper	40	62	5·4	4·5	0	34	0·6	50	0	0·09	1·2	0	250
Salmon, canned	0	48	5·7	2·8	0	85	0·4	70	0·01	0·06	1·8	0	170
Sardine, canned in oil	0	84	5·7	6·8	0	114	1·1	80	0·01	0·08	1·3	0	280
Shellfish, crab, lobster	60	34	5·7	1·1	0·3	13	0·3	0	0·03	0·07	2·5	0	0

* of this 26 mg. is in the U.K. added as calcium carbonate.

** of this 35 mg. is in the U.K. added as calcium carbonate.

† the vitamin content varies with the season and the way the cow is fed.

†† margarines may be fortified to different degrees; for the bakery trade margarine is not fortified at all.

THE NUTRITIVE COMPOSITION OF REPRESENTATIVE SAMPLES OF VARIOUS FOODS—continued

	Waste	Calories	Protein	Fat	Carbo-hydrate	Calcium	Iron	Vitamin A	Vitamin B1	Ribo-flavin	Niacin	Vitamin C	Vitamin D
	%		g.	g.	g.	mg.	mg.	i.u.	mg.	mg.	mg.	mg.	i.u.
5. Meat													
Bacon	12	128	3·1	12·8	0	3	0·3	0	0·17	0·06	0·3	0	0
Beef, corned	0	69	7·1	4·5	0	3	3·1	0	0	0·04	0·5	0	0
Beef, average quality	17	89	4·2	8·0	0	3	1·1	14	0·02	0·07	1·3	0	0
Beef, stewing	25	60	4·8	4·5	0	3	1·1	14	0·02	0·07	1·3	0	0
Chicken	30	38	5·1	2·0	0	3	1·0	0	0·04	0·03	2·3	0	0
Kidney	0	36	4·5	2·0	0	3	3·8	300	0·07	0·37	3·8	0	0
Liver, ox	0	40	4·8	1·7	1·4	3	3·9	4000	0·11	0·85	3·8	0	0
Mutton, lamb, average quality	17	94	3·7	8·8	0	3	0·6	14	0·04	0·05	1·2	0	0
Pork	15	116	3·4	11·4	0	3	0·3	0	0·20	0·06	1·7	0	0
Rabbit	17	38	5·7	1·6	0	3	0·6	0	0·01	0·14	1·8	0	0
Sausages, beef	0	61	3·3	3·7	3·7	9	0·6	0	0·04	0·02	0·5	0	0
Sausages, pork	0	73	3·0	5·1	3·7	9	0·3	0	0·04	0·03	1·0	0	0
Sweetbreads	40	68	6·2	4·5	0	18	0·4	10	0·09	0·03	3·6	0	0
Tongue, canned	0	73	5·4	5·7	0	3	0·9	0	0·08	0·03	1·0	0	0
Tripe	45	17	3·3	0·3	0	20	0·2	10	0·05	0·03	1·0	0	0
Veal	27	36	5·1	1·7	0	3	0·6	15	0·02	0·04	2·0	0	0
6. Vegetables													
Beans, broad	75	20	2·0	0·1	2·7	8	0·3	0	0·05	0·04	0·3	8	0
Beans, French	5	4	0·3	0	0·7	9	0·2	60	0·02	0·03	0·1	3	0
Beans, baked, canned	0	25	1·7	0	4·5	16	0·7	0	0·02	0·01	0·2	0	0
Beans, haricot, uncooked	0	71	6·1	0	11·6	51	1·9	0	0·13	0·08	0·6	0	0
Beetroot, boiled	0	12	0·5	0	2·5	8	0·2	0	0·01	0·02	0·1	2	0
Brussels sprouts	25	10	1·2	0	1·1	8	0·3	40	0·03	0·02	0·1	28	0
Cabbage	30	7	0·4	0	1·4	18	0·3	90	0·02	0·02	0·1	20	0
Carrot	5–20	6	0·2	0	0·8	14	0·2	1700	0·02	0·01	0·2	3	0
Cauliflower	30	6	0·7	0	1·1	14	0·4	0	0·03	0·02	0·2	20	0
Leeks	50	7	0·7	0	1·1	11	0·4	70	0·03	0·02	0·2	6	0
Lentils	0	82	6·8	0	13·6	11	2·2	0	0·13	0·02	0·9	0	0
Lettuce	20	3	0·3	0	0·5	7	0·2	400	0·02	0·02	0·1	4	0
Onion	5	6	0·3	0	1·3	9	0·1	0	0·01	0·01	0·1	3	0
Peas, green	60	17	1·6	0	2·7	14	0·5	50	0·12	0·03	0·2	8	0

Food													
Potatoes	7-25	21	0·6	0	4·6	2	0·2	0	0·03	0·02	0·3	2-8‡	0
Spinach	15	6	0·8	0	0·7	20	0·9	1200	0·03	0·06	0·1	18	0
Tomato	15	4	0·3	0	1·0	4	0·1	300	0·02	0·01	0·3	7	0
Turnip	35	5	0·2	0	1·0	17	0·1	0	0·01	0·01	0·3	7	0
Watercress	15	4	0·8	0	0·2	63	0·4	500	0·03	0·02	0·5	17	0
7. Fruit													
Apple	20	12	0·1	0	3·0	1	0·1	0	0·01	0·01	0·1	1	0
Apricot, dried	40	50	1·4	0	11·1	26	1·2	500	0	0·12	0·6	0	0
Banana	0	21	0·3	0	4·9	2	0·1	10	0·01	0·01	0·2	3	0
Blackberry	0	8	0·4	0	1·6	18	0·3	30	0·01	0·01	0·1	6	0
Blackcurrant	14	8	0·3	0	1·7	17	0·4	10	0·01	0·01	0·1	60	0
Dates	0	68	0·6	0	16·3	19	1·2	10	0	0·08	0·5	0	0
Figs, dried	0	58	1·0	0	13·5	81	0·2	20	0·01	0·08	0·1	0	0
Gooseberries	50	10	0·2	0	2·4	5	0·1	20	0·01	0·01	0·1	11	0
Grapes	25	17	0·2	0	4·1	5	0·1	0	0·02	0·01	0·1	1	0
Grapefruit	30	6	0·2	0	1·4	5	0·1	5	0·01	0·01	0·1	14	0
Lemon	25	5	0·2	0	0·8	20	0·1	0	0·01	0·01	0·1	12	0
Orange	6	10	0·2	0	2·2	12	0·1	30	0·01	0·01	0·1	16	0
Pineapple, canned	20	7	0·1	0	4·9	11	0·1	5	0·01	0·01	0·2	3	0
Plums	17	5	0·2	0	1·6	4	0·2	40	0	0·01	0·6	1	0
Prunes, dried	8	44	0·7	0	10·3	17	0·8	250	0·04	0·04	0·1	0	0
Raisins, dried	7	67	0·3	0	16·5	12	0·5	5	0·01	0·01	0·2	0	0
Raspberries		7	0·3	0	1·4	29	0·3	10	0·01	0·01	0·1	9	0
Rhubarb	25	2	0·2	0	0·3	6	0·1	0	0	0·01	0·1	3	0
Strawberries	3	7	0·2	0	1·6		0·2	0	0·01	0·01	0·1	17	0
8. Nuts													
Almonds	65	164	5·8	15·2	1·1	70	1·2	0	0·07	0·05	0·4	0	0
Brazil nuts	55	177	3·9	17·5	1·0	50	0·8	0	0·30	0·05	0·4	0	0
Chestnuts	20	47	0·6	0·8	9·3	13	0·3	0	0·06	0·05	0·4	0	0
Peanuts	30	166	8·0	13·9	2·2	17	0·7	0	0·25	0·08	0·6	0	0
Walnuts	40	151	3·5	14·6	1·3	17	0·7	0	0·08	0·05	0·4	0	0
9. Sugar, sweets and preserves													
Chocolate, plain	0	148	1·3	9·2	15·0	7	0·9	0	0·03	0·07	0·3	0	0
Honey	0	78	0·1	0	19·5	1	0·1	0	0	0·02	0·1	0	0
Jam	0	71	0·1	0	17·6	3	0·3	0	0	0	0	3	0
Sugar	0	108	0	0	27·0	0	0	0	0	0	0	0	0
Syrup, golden	0	81	0·1	0	20·2	7	0·4	0	0	0	0	0	0
Treacle, black	0	70	0·3	0	17·2	70	2·6	0	0·02	0·02	1·1	0	0

‡ the vitamin C content falls steadily during the months of storage.

The Nutritive Composition of Representative Samples of Various Foods—continued

	Waste	Calories	Protein	Fat	Carbo-hydrate	Calcium	Iron	Vitamin A	Vitamin B_1	Ribo-flavin	Niacin	Vitamin C	Vitamin D
	%		g.	g.	g.	mg.	mg.	i.u.	mg.	mg.	mg.	mg.	i.u.
10 *Beverages*													
Beer, bitter	0	16	0·1	0	(2·6)	1	0	0	0	0·02	0·4	0	0
Beer, mild	0	10	0·1	0	(1·5)	3	0	0	0	0·01	0·4	0	0
Cocoa, beverage as drunk	0	6	0·2	0·2	0·9	3	0	3	0		0	0	0
Cocoa, powder	0	125	5·8	7·3	8·9	14	4·1	15	0·03	0·08	0·3	0	0
Tea, beverage as drunk	0	5	0·1	0·1	0·8	3	0	4	0	0	0	0	0
Whisky	0	70	0	0	(9·9)	0	0	0	0	0	0	0	0

INDEX